A Different Kind of Strong will take you on a spiritual journey. It is a real account of deliverance, a kind of Saint Augustine conversion from a life of sin to one of devotion to God. Readers are likely to draw comfort and inspiration from Daniel L. Trotter's story and from the courage he shows by being willing to share it. - Francesca R.

This story encourages readers to take a lesson from the valuable outcomes that Daniel had in overcoming his life's obstacles. - Edward F.

Daniel's story will keep readers engaged. The foreword and afterword help bind the story like bookends, ensuring that readers know that what they are about to enjoy is not a simple autobiography but a narrative of redemption. It took a great deal of endurance to turn his life around, but he never dwells on his own courage or strength but rather gives credit where credit is due—to God. While Daniel has made his way out of the wilderness, he has not forgotten what it was like to walk that lonely road.
- Sandra C.

Pay attention to this memoir! It is full of dramatic "dark side" action and some equally dramatic turnarounds as Daniel mends his ways. This isn't just a turnaround tale but is also a love story. – Ben L.

A Different
Kind of Strong

A Different Kind of Strong

Daniel L. Trotter

© 2016 Daniel L. Trotter
All rights reserved. No part of this book may be reproduced in any form or by any means without written permission from the author.

A Different Kind of Strong by Daniel L. Trotter
© By Intellectual Reserve, Inc.
This publication is neither made, provided, approved, nor endorsed by Intellectual Reserve, Inc. or The Church of Jesus Christ of Latter-day Saints. Any content or opinions expressed, implied or included in or with the publication are solely those of the owner and not those of Intellectual Reserve, Inc. or The Church of Jesus Christ of Latter-day Saints.

ISBN: 1537627031
ISBN 13: 9781537627038
Library of Congress Control Number: 2016915204
CreateSpace Independent Publishing Platform
North Charleston, South Carolina

*To my loving wife, Julianne,
I appreciate all of your support and many sacrifices which have made this book possible. Thank you for believing in me, and loving me like no one else ever has. My sincerest gratitude to my family and many friends who have helped me along my journey. Most importantly, I would like to thank my Heavenly Father and His Son, Jesus Christ, my Savior, for saving me.*

Contents

Foreword · xi

Chapter 1	The Path to Addiction · · · · · · · · · · · · · · · ·	1
Chapter 2	Meth Takes Over · · · · · · · · · · · · · · · · · · ·	10
Chapter 3	The Fear of Death · · · · · · · · · · · · · · · · · ·	18
Chapter 4	Total Confusion ·	25
Chapter 5	Loss of Hope ·	30
Chapter 6	Mind, Body, Spirit · · · · · · · · · · · · · · · · · ·	36
Chapter 7	The Fast ·	48
Chapter 8	The Comeback ·	60
Chapter 9	A New Life ·	66
Chapter 10	Honesty, Friendship, and Love · · · · · · · · · ·	77
Chapter 11	Surpassing Expectations · · · · · · · · · · · · · ·	83
Chapter 12	Finally and Forever · · · · · · · · · · · · · · · · · ·	88
Chapter 13	The Reasons for Adversity · · · · · · · · · · · · ·	95

Afterword · 109
Author Bio ·115

Foreword
by Julianne Trotter

On October 14, 2011, Daniel Trotter began a forty-day fast. He was consumed by a question and desperate to know, *what do I do?* After thirty days in the wilderness, God sent him home with an answer. It was, "Come back to Me."

Today is the three-year anniversary of this event, and oh, how his life has changed. Miracles upon miracles have taken place. His road has not been easy, but it has been worth every step. For earnest seekers, only the truth of all things will satisfy a consuming desire for honest and specific answers from heaven. The story you are about to read is true. Although some names were changed, the people are real, and the events really happened. Daniel's life is a marvelous work of God—and nothing short of a miracle!

A year ago today, Daniel was living in Spokane, Washington, with his father. He had recommitted himself to the full service of God—in heart and deed—and to The Church of Jesus Christ of Latter-day Saints (LDS). He was once again ordained a priest, and his ward's elders quorum received him in full fellowship. He received a church calling to be a teacher in the Primary. Life seemed good at the time. Little did he know, with a little faith, patience, and determination, life would become even better.

Daniel had been writing songs of the heart for several years. They had one purpose: to glorify God, our loving Father. He sang and played his guitar as tribute for his personal miracles. He could not deny them, and he wanted to do something to express his gratitude to his Father in heaven. So he began to sing about what he learned through his experiences.

==He sang about Jesus Christ and what a lonely road He must have walked.== He sang about his own life's experiences, taking an honest look at his past and the consequences he faced for his decisions. He was a new man now. He knew it was not his own doing but because of saving grace—because of Jesus Christ.

Most of his music was solemn and weighty. There was a heaviness about his sound and the lyrics. He didn't sugarcoat his journey through the darkness in his personal wilderness. It was raw, unfiltered, and as honest and pure as his feelings could be. To listen to his music was to hear the depth of his yearning and the sincerity of his soul.

I don't know the series of events that prompted Daniel to pack up his life and few belongings and drive to Salt Lake City with his guitar. I don't know what made him think that something better was going to happen there. Why risk going

A Different Kind of Strong

from good to unknown, from a safe and wholesome community to a new life? What I do know is that his brave and bold decision to do that impacted my life profoundly. It tested my faith to the core, forcing me to learn about atonement and forgiveness, mercy, and grace. Because of Daniel's decision, I have learned how important each of us is to God. We really matter to Him. Our Father in heaven and Jesus Christ love us without cause or condition. It just "is." I have learned about true friendship and having pure love for someone else—even a complete stranger.

As I write this foreword, I wonder what was going on in Daniel's mind when he moved. What was he doing each day? What were his goals and dreams? Was he preparing for a new chapter in his life? If so, how? What made him happy? He has said that happiness is a choice we make; therefore, I know that he was already happy before we met. I know that I don't "make" him happy. Instead, I strive to enhance his happiness by showing him patience, appreciation, respect, validation, and tenderness. I love him, every day.

As you read Daniel's story, know that there is another story to follow already. This story is unwritten because it is unfolding every day. It is alive and growing as Daniel and I share the adventure of faith together. I invite you to read on. Begin with Daniel's journey. Learn from his experiences at a safe distance. Try to understand the difficult lessons, hard earned for him. Perhaps he will be an example of how to avoid our own darkness; perhaps it will help us begin again. It is never too late.

If we are willing to let God guide us, we are exactly where we need to be right now. If we are willing, we can become more aware or wake up to a greater and better understanding of ourselves, who and what we are, and of God's plan for us and His willingness to lead us along the path we must take back to Him. This is the road less traveled. Welcome, fellow seeker of truth and peace. I hope you enjoy this story of high adventure. May it encourage you to begin an adventure of your own. It is worth every step, and as the poet Robert Frost wrote of two roads,

I took the one less traveled by,
And that has made all the difference.

CHAPTER 1
THE PATH TO ADDICTION

I SMOKED MY FIRST CIGARETTE when I was seven years old. It was just a cigarette, right? How much harm could it do? ==That's the way addiction gets a hold of you: little by little.==

Next came self-gratification. We talk about pornography a lot, but not the act that goes with it. This is a very real and very destructive behavior in our society. Engaging in this selfish and destructive act was an addiction that took me decades to overcome.

Then one day, my siblings and I received some disturbing news. My parents were getting a divorce. Now, don't get me wrong. I'm not blaming my parents' divorce for the paths I chose. I take full responsibility for the decisions I have made.

After the divorce, I decided to live with my dad. Things went well when I was with him. I had always been one of nine kids before, but now it was just my dad and I, so we were able to spend a lot of time together.

Later, my two brothers moved with us to San Clemente, California. We met some of the locals—and let's just say they weren't a positive influence on us. To tell you the truth, I don't think we were a very positive influence on them either. This was when I started drinking alcohol and smoking marijuana.

My years in junior high were definitely rebellious ones. In the seventh grade, I was suspended fifteen times for a total of forty-five days. I was out of control. Drinking and smoking marijuana was just the beginning. I started to do crack, mushrooms, and LSD. I also got heavily into pornography. This was at the age of thirteen.

At age sixteen, I used methamphetamines for the first time. This was in 1991. Meth is one of the most (if not the single most) addictive and destructive drugs known to humanity. It didn't take complete control over my life at that point, but it would in my twenties.

My behavior in junior high continued in high school. During my freshman and sophomore years, I failed almost every class. I missed homework assignments and often skipped my classes. I didn't feel comfortable at this high school. I had heard of a continuation school nearby. Even though it might not sound like a positive solution, I thought it was a better fit for me. It was one of the best decisions I made in my younger years.

This new school was full of kids with many different problems, the kids whom most school systems just couldn't handle. For whatever reason, I became very comfortable there and felt it was the place I needed to be. My grades began to improve, and I quit smoking cigarettes. That was kind of odd, since I was at a school that allowed us to smoke. Yet I quit smoking for about three years.

Even though I was still participating in some drug activity and drinking alcohol, I was doing better. My reputation grew at school—not as the bad kid, like in junior high, but as a positive influence on the students. I had a wonderful teacher and counselor who encouraged me to run for class president. I didn't put much effort into my campaign, because I didn't think I would win, but I did. I became the high school's first senior-class president. That gave me the motivation to do better.

I started to take school seriously, and my grades improved dramatically. I put in the hard work and effort to complete the necessary credits, and I finished just two days before graduation. As senior-class president, I was interviewed by the local newspaper and asked to speak at the ceremony. I also received a scholarship (from a local company) honoring me for my achievements.

After high school, I started working. Because of that job, I started to have back problems. My uncle, who was a chiropractor, tried to help me, but over time, my problems got worse. I might have to deal with them for the rest of my life.

During this time, I was heavily into alcohol and cocaine. I used marijuana as well, but it made me think too much. I started getting very uncomfortable using it, so I didn't do it too often. These were addictions that were an everyday part of my life. As long as I was on drugs and alcohol, I would never live responsibly.

I was living with my friends Richard and Chris Rodriguez and their family when I received a phone call from one of my brothers. He wanted me to move to Santa Cruz, California, and live with him. I had visited him before and loved the area. After thinking about it for a time, I decided to make the move. I had no idea what I was getting into.

When I got to Santa Cruz, it felt like I was home. Everyone welcomed me like I was a native to the Westside. The Westside is a part of Santa Cruz where not many people can just walk in and be accepted. My brother had laid the foundation and knew a lot of people, so they welcomed me as one of their own.

It was very exciting to a young, struggling man. This new scene was similar to the one I had just left, but it was more hard core. More girls. More cocaine. More alcohol. There was always a reason to party. I thought, *This is the life. This is living.*

I met so many people and got to hang out with lots of beautiful girls. I even had the opportunity to meet many professional surfers. Several of them became my closest friends. I also met a couple of NFL football players and a well-known professional baseball player.

It was a very easy and exciting life. People started to accept me and consider me a friend. The people I knew felt like one big family. That's what so many people are looking for—to be accepted and be a part of something. That's why some

==people will join anything. No matter what it is, they think it's better than being alone.==

Cocaine was a major feature of the party scene in Santa Cruz. The best way to have an unlimited supply was to sell it, which is exactly what my brother and I started doing. We began to be known as reliable sources. We were always "holding," which meant we always had some in our possession. My brother's best friend, Charlie, helped us get a steady clientele. We partied and made money doing it.

One day, we received an opportunity to do a major drug deal. It would make us some money, and we would receive a good amount of coke as our cut. It was kind of like a finder's fee. The deal was for a kilo of coke (just over two pounds). Its street value was about $80,000. We were middlemen, getting this purchase for a friend.

A deal like this doesn't happen overnight. There's a lot of preparation and footwork that needs to be done. You have to contact your supplier. The buyer needs to negotiate. Several meetings need to take place just to set the deal up.

We thought we were big-timers. We were spending a lot of money at the bars on alcohol. We really thought we were something. One time at a bar, we acted like we were fighting over who would pay the tab as we flashed hundred-dollar bills. We were yelling out, "I'm buying! No, I'm buying. You paid last time!" We were just drawing attention to ourselves, acting like we had a lot of money. But we didn't.

The day came when the big deal was to go down. I had just gotten off work doing construction and stopped by Charlie's house. My brother and I lived down the hall from Charlie's apartment. When I got to his place, he greeted me at the door with excitement. He was also a little bit anxious. "We're about to do this," Charlie said. I entered the apartment and saw my brother sitting on the couch. Charlie's guy, the supplier, was there too. All three of them were packing guns. They explained the situation to me.

I decided to go home and shower really quick, but I said I would be back right after. "If anything happens, take this, and be prepared," Charlie told me as he handed me a gun. To this day, I don't even know what type of gun it was. Guns were never my thing. But I took it with me.

I jumped in the shower, and just before I was done, I heard a knock. I threw a towel around my waist and opened the door. It was one of my neighbors. She asked, "What's going on at Charlie's? There are cops everywhere!"

I got dressed as quickly as I could, left the gun, and ran down to see what was going on. Sure enough, the Santa Cruz Police Department and FBI, FDA, and ATF agents had swarmed the whole apartment building. They had busted down Charlie's door and had taken in the group for questioning. As I was waiting, I wondered if they knew who I was. I sat out front, patiently waiting as they started bringing everyone out—Charlie, his supplier, then my brother. Funny thing was that our "friend" and his buddy, the buyer, were nowhere to be seen. Obviously, something was up.

As I waited, I got paranoid. Were they going to raid my apartment too? I remembered we had about a pound of pot in my closet. I didn't know what to do, so I called Charlie's brother, Oscar. I told him what had happened. I also told him about the pot in my house. We decided to take it to his house when things calmed down. That was a risky move, but we thought it was necessary.

We later learned that our "friend" had been in trouble with the law several times. He had been in prison twice and was on his third strike. (California had recently passed the three-strikes law.) He was looking at twenty-five years to life. He had a family, and he wasn't willing to do his time, so he had "rolled over" on his friends. The cops had made a deal with him. If he would set up a big drug bust for them, they would alter the charges against him.

Even after all that, we still didn't stop partying, but we did slow down. After some legal counseling, Charlie, my brother, and their lawyer negotiated an agreement. They would each get three years in prison by pleading no contest (only eighteen months if they maintained good behavior) instead of seven if they both pled not guilty and would have lost their case. That sounds pretty dramatic for a drug deal, but the firearms factor had bumped the sentencing up to severe.

I read the reports and saw my name in all of them. I was at all the meetings that took place. I was a suspect, like the rest of them. But because I wasn't at the actual drug bust, there was nothing they could do. They couldn't bring me into court. They couldn't question me. They couldn't do anything. I now know that this was definitely a tender mercy from God. I don't know how I would've handled prison back then. My friends were from all different races, so I probably wouldn't have followed the inmate's rules of sticking to your own kind. That would've been very dangerous for me, so I think God saved me from that fate.

Realizing that my brother would be gone for a while, I decided to go back to Southern California and to live with Chris Rodriguez and his uncle in East Los Angeles. This was not the safest place to be. East LA is known for an extremely high crime rate, and it is saturated with gang activity. Sometimes it felt like I was the only white guy around. Things weren't too bad though. I knew my friends had my back.

Chris and I commuted to San Clemente for work, but we partied in LA. It was all about sports, alcohol, and lots of cocaine. That's what our life was about. We often played basketball too. That was probably the only healthy thing we did.

After several months, Chris and I decided to move back to San Clemente, but that didn't change a thing. Everywhere I went, I surrounded myself with others who were just like me. Life was all about drugs, alcohol, sports, and girls. Soon, though, I got laid off. But I had the opportunity to live in Las Vegas with Chris's brother, Richard, and the rest of their family. Once again I was on the move.

Vegas was a partier's dream: cheap drinks, gambling (which was never really my thing), and strip clubs. There always seemed to be something to do. That town literally does not sleep. I worked in construction there but then started working as a cook. At one point, I had three jobs. Some days, I worked from six in the morning until eleven at night and then still went out to the bars and clubs to party. I'd get a few hours of sleep and then do it all over again. That was my life in Vegas. I don't know how my body made it.

In time, I got involved with Chris and Richard's younger sister. This did not go over well with them, and it fractured the relationship I had had with them for so many years. It wasn't like they hated me or like we weren't friends anymore; it was just that things became very different. I felt uncomfortable, and I'm sure they did too.

← Constantly moving in & out of alcohol and drugs.

CHAPTER 2
METH TAKES OVER

———∞∞∞———

TIMING IS EVERYTHING. MY BROTHER was released from prison, and I decided to return to Santa Cruz. I moved in with him, his wife, and his stepson. It didn't take too long for us to pick up where we had left off. My brother and I started going out while my sister-in-law and her kid stayed at home. Soon, my brother's wife did not want me around anymore. It was time for me to find a new place to live.

I ended up staying at Oscar Gonzalez's house. He was Charlie's brother. Oscar and I became very close friends. We went out and did everything together—namely, the same routine: alcohol, drugs, and girls.

One night at a party, we got into a heated conversation with a few gang members. They were harassing a couple of girls we knew, so we went to Oscar's house and picked up some baseball bats. Then we went back. That's when I learned you don't bring a bat to a gunfight.

They pulled out their guns and took our bats. One of them grabbed me and put the gun to my back. He kept threatening to kill me over and over again. I got so sick of hearing it that I told him to go ahead and pull the trigger. I don't think he was expecting to hear that.

I heard someone in the background say, "Danny, look out!" As I turned to look, one of the gang members hit me in the head with a bat. I was startled and not sure what had happened, but I was still totally conscious and never went down. I was wearing a beanie, and I think it saved my life or prevented me from severe brain damage.

My head was completely split open, though, and bleeding profusely. My beanie was full of blood, and so was my sweater. The cops showed up and tried to get me into the ambulance to go to the hospital, but I had no insurance, so I declined. I answered all their questions correctly, so they had to let me go. They couldn't force me into the vehicle.

An hour or so later, I ended up going to the ER myself and got stitched up. The knob on my head was the size of a baseball—that is no exaggeration. I was lucky to be alive.

Despite this incident, I returned to the same old things: drugs, alcohol, and girls. To be honest, I had always been terrified of girls. I trace this back to when I was about five years old when I was caught naked under the bed with a friend of the family's daughter. We didn't know what we were doing; we were just exploring. But that made my mom and dad furious. I received a severe spanking and more punishment for it. For years, I subconsciously believed that women equaled pain. That made it hard for

me to communicate with them. I needed alcohol to do that. It gave me confidence.

Oscar lived in a small bedroom in his parents' house. Although I was grateful for his hospitality, it was too small for the both of us, so I ended up renting a room from one of our friends, a guy named Rudy. This guy was known for hooking up with lots of girls. What do you know? Another place to party.

I also started hanging out with a guy named Alan, whom I had met through some of our friends. Alan was a character. I had never met anyone like him before, and I have yet to meet someone like him since. We became best friends and went everywhere together. We drank a lot of Jack Daniel's with very little Coke in it, but we did a lot of cocaine.

Unfortunately, at this point, my brother's wife divorced him. When you live the life that we lived, nothing seems to last. Shortly, we were roommates again and got back into dealing coke. Our house became the place to party. This was when I met Tracy. She was the first girl I had deep feelings for. We started dating, but that didn't mean she was faithful. Before we met, she already had problems, and I did not make her life any easier. I was getting back into meth and introduced her to it. Meth did not help with her issues.

Then I met Bruce. Bruce was a pretty intimidating guy. My best friend, Alan, introduced us because Bruce and I both played guitar. We started to make some pretty cool music. Bruce had never done meth. I introduced him to it too. That was a bad idea. A guy like Bruce had enough anger

A Different Kind of Strong

and hatred in him already; he didn't need anything to enhance it. I have to admit, though, that when I saw him with his daughter, I could see who he truly was—a kind and loving person. But it was the only time I saw him act that way.

A lot of us started doing meth. I had experience with it, and I knew what could potentially happen. I remember telling Alan and Bruce that this stuff was going to tear us apart and ruin our lives. That's exactly what happened. Everyone became very suspicious and distrustful.

One night, I was drawing a picture for an album cover for the band Bruce and I wanted to start. I was up all night working on it. At about six in the morning, my other brother, who had just moved in with us, came into my room and told me to come see what was on the TV. That day was September 11, 2001. The Twin Towers had just been hit by terrorist-piloted commercial jets. I was stunned. Not just because of what happened, but also because of the picture I had drawn. I showed my brother, and he too was astonished.

My picture showed the world with the United States in the center with a huge explosion on it. From that day forward, my life would never be the same again. That was when things became very strange, and it was like something started to speak to me through people, television, music, and in several other ways.

When I showed Bruce my picture, the look on his face was like he had seen a ghost. I think I kind of freaked him out. Our relationship changed. I don't know if it was because of the drugs or because of the picture—probably a little of both. He became real secretive, and that made me paranoid. Everything became weird...things I did in daily life then came up in conversation, on the radio, or on TV. It was like I was on *The Truman Show*, and I was Jim Carrey.

When you're on meth, you don't know what's real and what is your mind playing tricks on you. I'm sure I was paranoid, but at the same time, I knew there were some weird things going on with my friends, especially Bruce. I didn't trust him anymore.

At this point, meth had completely taken over my life. I had no job and no money. Because one of my brothers had lost his job, my other brother was paying the bills, and it got to a point to where he couldn't support us any longer. He decided to move out. When that happened, we had to move out as well. We were both homeless.

We rented hotels occasionally, but mostly we stayed at our friends' houses. Basically, we wandered from drug house to drug house. For a little while, I was able to stay at Tracy's mom's house until I told her parents that we were on meth. They asked what was wrong with their daughter, and I told them, thinking that maybe they could help us get clean. Tracy didn't like that very much and threw all my clothes out on the front lawn. I was homeless again.

Shortly after this, Tracy announced that she was pregnant. To this day, I don't know if it was really my child. She thought it was, but she was not the type of person who could be trusted. Even though I didn't believe I was the father, I accepted that an abortion was the best option. This didn't feel good to me, but I also knew I was in no position to raise and support a child.

With me homeless, Tracy getting an abortion, Bruce being shady, and the rest of my friends not approving of what I was doing, I decided to move back to San Clemente. I remember crying on the drive there because I missed Tracy. I had never felt that kind of heartache before. It didn't feel good leaving her behind.

The paranoia and memories from Santa Cruz didn't stay in Santa Cruz. I was always looking over my shoulder and wondering if people were watching me. I wasn't convinced that it was just because of the drugs.

Returning to San Clemente was hard. I missed Tracy a lot. I was trying to work, but it was tough because I kept imagining what she was doing in Santa Cruz with all of my male friends. It was driving me nuts, to where I could barely function. Those thoughts consumed me throughout the day. I was angry and became very bitter toward women.

I went off meth for a little while but not for long. I got together with some old friends and started drinking, and that led to wanting to use meth again. My brother, the one I had been homeless with, had moved back to San Clemente before me. We were both living with my dad now, and we had started working with him in construction. We were making decent money but blowing it on drugs and alcohol. That meant trouble.

One night, my brother and I were at a bar. Some guys came in and sat near us. We overheard them saying they were going to jump us. We just laughed. All of them left, except for one guy. He came up and told us we were lucky. I asked why. He said that they were planning to jump us. I said, "Why would you want to do that? You would just get knocked out." He walked away, calling me a name I didn't like, so I followed him outside. I asked him what he had said, and he turned around.

I remembered something in that moment that Bruce had taught me. He showed me how to knock someone out in a single punch, and that is exactly what I did. All the anger I had built up over the years came out of me in that one punch. I hit him so hard that I split his chin wide open, and he fell forward as I brushed him to the side of me. As he fell to the ground, I said, "I told you that you were going to get knocked out."

The bartender came out yelling, "We don't do that here!"

I said, "Tonight, you do." I was so angry and full of adrenaline in that moment. Then I felt bad. I wished it had never happened. We quickly left, fearing the cops might come.

After a while, my dad had had enough of our behavior, and so had my stepmom. They kicked us out. There we were again, back on the street, going house to house and hotel to hotel, sleeping in a car at times, and just trying to find another place to get high and to party and hang out with girls. I look back at this time in my life, and I am amazed at the things I used to do. My life is so different now. It's like night and day.

A Different Kind of Strong

I started thinking about my life, what it had become, and what was I going to do about it. I had a warrant back in Santa Cruz for drinking and driving. I knew my life could not go forward without resolving this issue. Although I was not sober, I decided to go up to Santa Cruz and do the time for it.

Before I left San Clemente, though, I bought two grams of meth. I took it on the plane with me. That was risky, but when you're a drug addict, it doesn't matter. I knew I was going to be sober soon, so I was going to party it up before I went to jail.

[handwritten note: Constantly moving, partying and getting in fights]

CHAPTER 3

THE FEAR OF DEATH

—⊗⊗⊗—

MY BEST FRIEND, ALAN, PICKED me up from the airport. I stayed with him for a week and partied at his place. After the meth was all gone, I was off to the Santa Cruz courthouse. I told the judge I had nothing to offer but my time; I had no money to pay off the fine. The judge gave me forty-five days. I agreed to the terms, and he told me to turn myself in at the Santa Cruz County Jail the next day.

I spent a couple of days at the jail and then was transferred to "the Farm." Another name for it was "Camp Snoopy." It was still jail, but it was kind of a walk in the park. Just a bunch of guys in bunks out in the middle of nowhere. There were no fences. You could leave whenever you wanted. But if you did, you would pay the price by doing more time when you were caught.

Time went by; it wasn't bad. I got to eat, sleep, and do some work release. This kept my mind off where I was and gave me a little bit of freedom. Although it wasn't much, it was better than staying at the facility all day.

It's funny how people think that they are real tough or "hard." Some of the guys there acted like they were in traditional prison. A group of white inmates gathered the other white guys and told them to "stick to their own." They said, "Don't buy cigarettes from anybody outside of your race." I laughed inside at how ridiculous that was and walked away from the group. I got along with everyone. I had a couple of Mexican friends there, and I wasn't going to turn my back on them just because a couple of wannabes thought they were in San Quentin. This is why if I had gone to prison, I probably would have gotten a beatdown or even been killed.

I spent the holidays in there. It was good. I didn't mind it. I just wanted to get that warrant taken care of, and at the same time, I was getting sober. After twenty-eight days, I was released for good behavior, and I was on my way to sobriety.

I went back to Alan's house for a few days and tried to get healthier. I started doing a little running and taking care of myself. That was when I met a girl named Helen through some old friends of mine. They drank, but they didn't do any hard drugs. I went out with them to the bars but didn't drink.

Helen and I started to become very close. We liked each other a lot. She was a fun girl with a good heart. That was probably the first real sober relationship I ever had. It was different, for sure. But I thought it was time to go back to San Clemente. I was able to move back in with my dad and stepmom. My brother had moved back in with them as well. We both started working with my dad again and saving money.

Helen and I talked on the phone often. She really wanted to be with me, and I wanted to be with her. She came to San Clemente and picked me up so I could move back to Santa Cruz. By that time, I was a couple of months sober and thought I had a handle on my addiction.

When I got to Santa Cruz, I actually did pretty well for a while. I got another job in construction and made good money. Things were looking great until one day, Helen said she was not interested in having a relationship with me anymore. I was furious. I had moved all the way back to Santa Cruz to be with her, and she had dropped me like a bad habit. That didn't go over well with me.

All it took was a little anger and one shot of Jack Daniel's, and I was right back where I had started. All in one night, I had lost my girl, started drinking again, and got right back on meth. You can guess what happened next.

I was living in a little studio in the back of a friend's house. Everyone that lived there did meth, so it was easy to get. I was getting myself back into the same old situation. I decided to move to a different place to get cleaned up, but my emptiness, fear, and anger just followed me there.

I tried to work and get things done, but my performance was definitely lacking. I was also losing a lot of weight. My boss could tell something was up, but he kept me around and even got me some side jobs so I could make more money. For one job, part of my payment was a car that had been sitting around for years but was in very good condition.

A Different Kind of Strong

That was about the time I started hanging out with Hector. I had met Hector a long time before, but we had never hung out regularly. He was the type of guy who was always in and out of prison. He was a gang member (a red-ragger or *Norteño*) and was the most feared person on the Westside. He even put fear into Bruce—and Bruce was pretty crazy himself. My brother and other friends tried to convince me it was a bad idea to hang out with Hector, but I didn't listen.

Hector and I hung out all the time. We even started working together. We went out a lot and became really good friends—almost inseparable. I was also hanging out with a girl named Leslie. We were not dating, but we did see each other a lot. Bruce was around here and there too, but I still didn't trust him. He was trying to get me to stay away from Hector as well, but I trusted Hector more than I did him. After a while, though, I didn't trust any of them.

One night I went to Rudy's house—he was my old roommate—to get some meth. After I returned home, I tried the stuff, and it was very weak. He obviously cut his dope a lot. I mentioned this to Hector, who got upset. He said, "Let's go over there and get what you paid for!" I was very hesitant, but I went anyway.

Hector knocked on the door, and Rudy answered. Hector went in and started acting crazy. He told Rudy it wasn't cool to rip me off, and he wanted to know where he kept his stash. Rudy showed him where it was. Hector didn't take all of it, but he did take what I paid for, and a bit more for the hassle. Everyone in the house was scared. Nobody wanted to mess with Hector, and because I was with him, nobody wanted to mess with me.

After Hector got the drugs and pumped fear into everyone, we left. I felt bad about the whole situation. I didn't feel right about what had just happened, but I also felt like I had gotten ripped off, and that wasn't right either. Because Rudy was a local, many people found out and then totally despised me. They wanted me gone. They had been my friends, but many of them turned their backs. I guess I can see why.

That night, Hector and I went back to my studio apartment. I fell asleep. Yeah, that's how good the stuff was—so good that I fell asleep. Hector woke me up, telling me somebody was outside, messing with my car. When we went out, we saw that a tire was on fire, and some of the windows were busted. I was so mad. I wanted to fight these guys. I thought they were cowards for going after my car instead of confronting me.

Later, I found out that there was a plan to get rid of me. A friend called to say that she had heard that a contract had been put out on me. People were willing to pay someone to kill me. That put me in a whole new world of fear. Talk about being paranoid. From then on, wherever I went, I was very cautious. At times, I carried a steak knife with me just to protect myself.

A friend named Kelly who had heard about the situation talked me into visiting her a couple of hours away. I thought it was a good idea—not just to get away, but because I also really liked her. She said she knew some people who might be able to protect me.

Once there, I got some sleep and sobered up. We met with her friends and had a long conversation about the people who wanted me dead. They said they could help. We decided a few of them would go down to Santa Cruz and tell those people to leave me alone.

When I got back home to Santa Cruz after my stay with Kelly, things seemed to be fine. I guess her friends' plan had worked. The people in Santa Cruz probably wondered how I had those kinds of connections. It was news to me too! I didn't even know that I had such influences. But thank goodness Kelly had called me that day.

The people who were after me now accepted that they couldn't touch me, but that didn't mean they had to like me. I had ruined my reputation and friendships. Many people didn't want me around anymore. I had lost all their trust and respect. But even after all of that, I still didn't quit doing meth.

One day, Kelly called to see how I was doing. I told her I was still using, and she was so frustrated with me that she hung up the phone and didn't talk to me anymore. After all of her help, I was back to the same old thing.

At that point, I was scared, paranoid, lost, and totally confused. I wasn't sure exactly what to do, but I knew that I was no longer welcome in Santa Cruz. I decided to move. The great thing was that I chose to leave because I wanted to, not out of fear.

Before I left, two very important things happened. Number one, Hector came over and asked me if I wanted some meth. I said no, but he insisted and left some on the table. He said, "Do whatever you want with it." After he left, I immediately picked up the bag and flushed it down the toilet. That was the last time I saw meth. The second thing was that I threw all my pornography in the trash. Those two decisions changed my life. That was my turning point.

I talked to another one of my brothers, who lived with his wife in Arkansas. They told me I could live with them. I was on the move again, but this time was going to be different. The transformation was about to begin.

CHAPTER 4
TOTAL CONFUSION

MOVING FROM SANTA CRUZ TO Paragould, Arkansas, was a big culture shock. Not only was it different geographically but also socially. One thing I noticed while driving in Paragould was that people waved at me. I thought, *Why are they waving at me? I don't know them.* I guess they were just being nice. I felt welcome.

Shortly after moving in with my brother and sister-in-law, I found out that the neighbor next door did meth and was probably selling it. Even after moving over two thousand miles, I was still being confronted by methamphetamines. It was just a test to see if I was serious about changing my life. I would soon find out that there is opposition in all things.

I had been clean from drugs a little over a week before I got to Arkansas, but I still thought people were playing games with me. I continued to receive messages through television, radio, and social interactions. Although it seemed odd, it was leading me somewhere.

One night, I was lying in bed, ready to go to sleep when I started thinking of a girl named Mary from back in Santa Cruz. She had been seeing my best friend, Alan. I had never mentioned it to anyone, but I really liked her. I thought she was perfect. Mary had a great spirit. She was kind, gentle, and very loving, quiet, and humble. She was small, gorgeous, and half Mexican. I always had a thing for Mexican girls, and petite ones at that.

My mind began to put together its own puzzle of what I wanted. I reflected on everything that had happened the past few years, and I figured it had all been a setup to get me clean so I could be with Mary. Maybe my life wasn't being threatened. Maybe my friends had set the whole thing up to scare me so I would stop using.

As I started to believe Mary and I were going to be together, I was filled with great anticipation and excitement. She became my motivation. She made me want to continue to change my life and be better.

It's funny how quickly we will respond to get what we want. One morning, I woke up and decided to throw my cigarettes in the garbage. Just like that, I quit. I wanted to be the best that I could for her. But when you decide to change for the better, obstacles will come. I started getting sick. I got earaches and strep throat. In the past, alcohol and drugs got rid of those sicknesses, but that was out of the question now. My new life had begun.

I talked to Alan, and he told me Mary was pregnant. I assumed the baby was mine even though we had never had sex.

I thought that Leslie, a girl whom I had had sex with in Santa Cruz, had taken my sperm to impregnate Mary. Like I said, drugs do many strange things to the mind. I thought everyone was in on the game and that it was all for my own good. But wow, this was craziness. It made me think even more that people were following me and watching my every move.

One day, I was going through a lot. I started having major back problems, but I couldn't get medical attention because I had no insurance. Just another obstacle. The pain was horrible. It was hard to move, walk, or do any kind of activity. Basically, I was in bed most of the time, lying down.

I also missed Mary terribly. I thought that somehow, she was either going to get in touch with me or magically appear. It was torture. This eventually led to a total breakdown—I ended up crying and walking the streets. I asked God why He was tormenting me. I just wanted to know where Mary was and when we would be together.

While I was in this state of misery, my brother found me and took me to a pastor at a local Baptist church. He counseled with me and gave me a Bible. Once I started reading, it sucked me in, as if I were reading parts of my life. Whatever I read about, something similar happened the next day. Or I did something and then read about it in the Bible. I was living a very strange life. But it was all for a reason. Something was talking to me.

I started going to the Baptist church and continued reading the Bible. It helped me understand more about God and His son, Jesus Christ. This was my first step back into religion. I went to church every Sunday, most of the time by myself. While I was in Arkansas, I read the entire Bible. So many signs gave me hope.

I thought I had to wait three years before I could be with Mary. Even though this was a lot to take on, it seemed like plenty of time to get my life in order. My love for her gave me the will to endure. Let me clarify a little bit—maybe I didn't really love her; I just loved the idea of her. In my mind, she was this perfect little angel.

Soon, though, my back pain became so severe that I needed medical attention fast, so I went to see a neurologist. He told me I needed surgery right away. The doctor said he could do it if he had half of the money up front. But I had no money. That's when my mom helped me. She paid for half of the surgery so I could get back on my feet.

The operation was a complete success. When I woke up, my back and sciatic leg pain were gone. I remember walking to the bathroom just thirty minutes after my surgery. I went home just a few hours later.

As I spent time healing, I contemplated all the unhealthy things I had done to my body over the past twenty years. That was the moment my health and fitness journey began. Because I didn't have money to pay for physical therapy, I got a gym membership at a local hospital and started the rehabilitation process myself. I met with a personal trainer who gave me information on how to strengthen my back. I went to the gym daily, doing my best to get healthy.

A Different Kind of Strong

Mary continued to be my motivation to get healthy. My back healed up, and I started working out more and became more active. I even worked a little bit, but mostly, I was on unemployment. I was very grateful for it. It allowed me to pay bills as I healed.

After about eight months, I decided I didn't want to be in Arkansas anymore. Like I said, it was a big culture shock. I just didn't feel like I belonged there. So I called my mom, who lived in Richland, Washington, and decided to move there.

Moves to Paragould, AR

Gets into church

Has surgery on back

Leaves to Richland, WA

CHAPTER 5

Loss of Hope

Richland felt a lot more like home than Arkansas. It could've been because I was with my mom. She and my stepdad welcomed me into their home and helped me with whatever I needed.

I got a membership at a local gym and started working on a fitness program with a trainer. I wanted to be two hundred pounds of muscle. The trainer talked me into losing weight first and then going from there. She was absolutely right. I dropped about thirty pounds. Not only was I transforming my life, I was transforming my body.

I started running and spent hours in the gym, trying to strengthen my body. I began educating myself and asking trainers and other members for advice. It didn't take long for me to be hooked on health and fitness. The gym had a contest to see which team worked out the most. I wanted to give it my best. My longest day there was six and a half hours.

Soon, I got a job at one of the big chain grocery stores. They hired me as a cashier, but their goal was to put me into a management position. I went from cashier to the fourth person in charge of the store within two months. They quickly advanced me to journeyman pay because of my hard work. This was a miracle in itself, because this doesn't happen too often in the grocery industry.

I was doing well. I was working, supporting myself, and paying off debt. I also got my driver's license back. I hadn't had one since the DUI. Although things were going good, I had a long way to go. There were other areas in my life that needed attention.

As I improved, I felt compelled to start looking for a church. After attending a couple of different churches, I decided to go back to the LDS church because it just felt right. The last time I had been there was about twenty years earlier.

I received the Aaronic and then the Melchizedek priesthood and was called to be a second counselor in the elders quorum. But even though I was going church, I was still having many problems. I started counseling through the church and also saw an independent psychologist. I can see now that it was an important part of the process. I struggled, wondering if Mary and I were ever going to be together. I waited and waited, but nothing happened. Again, I thought she might appear one day, but she never did.

The pressure became intense. It affected my job, my social life, and just about everything I did, but somehow, I was able to work. My coworkers saw me as this healthy and happy guy, but little did they know how much I was struggling. The torment was so great that it put me in a psychiatric treatment center.

The doctors told me I was suffering from major depression. They put me on prescription drugs that my body utterly rejected. There was no real way for me to medicate, so I had to feel the experiences I was going through. I had to feel all the emotional and physical discomfort.

Although the psychiatric treatment center tried to help, it was not the answer for me. After a week, I was released and went back to work. I was trying to live a normal life, but I couldn't. The thought of Mary was a heavy burden. That's when I made the decision to drive down to Santa Cruz and talk to her.

The trip seemed to be for nothing. I talked to Alan, who was my best friend and still Mary's boyfriend. He said she didn't want to talk to me. He said she was scared of me because I was expressing that I loved her and she couldn't understand why. This devastated me. I was crushed.

While I was there, my brother told me that the guys who had pulled a gun on me and hit me in the head with a baseball bat years earlier were following him. I wasn't having that. I immediately jumped in the car and went to their house. I knocked on the door, and one of them answered. "Do you remember me?" I asked. I pointed at the scar on my forehead, where they had hit me with a bat.

He said, "Yeah, I remember you." I told him to stop messing with my brother, that my brother had nothing to do with our previous encounter. He denied that he was doing anything to my brother. I asked him if he wanted to take care of the situation then and there. I told him that we could settle this in his front yard, man to man. He didn't want to go there and didn't seem to think it was necessary.

I let him know that I was a different person and didn't party anymore. I told him I didn't even live there anymore and that he didn't have to worry about me ever again. I simply wanted them to leave my brother alone. I also wanted to make sure that everything was OK between us now, and he said it was. I said thanks, shook his hand, got into my car, and drove away. I've never seen him again. I think he respected me a lot more after that day.

Now that I had found out that Mary didn't want anything to do with me and I had settled a longtime grudge, I returned to Richland. I went back to work and tried to move on, but I couldn't. One night when I came home, it was all weighing heavily on me, and I had a breakdown—one of many. I had waited so long to be with Mary, I had changed so much over three years, and then I had found out we were never going to be together. This was so hard for me to accept that I just couldn't handle it.

One night when I got off work, I was distraught. My mom tried to comfort me, but the wounds were too deep. I sat in the dining room, evaluating my life. There seemed to be only one solution. It was time for me to leave this world. I didn't want to live anymore. I just wanted it to all go away. I wanted to go away. I thought that killing myself was the only way out.

At this point, my mom went to her room to call someone. I remember going into the kitchen and grabbing some sleeping pills. I can't remember how many I took. I just kept popping them, one after another. I went back to the dining room and sat down, and the pills started to kick in. My mom walked back in and noticed a change in my behavior. I remember her asking, "What did you do? Danny, what did you do?"

She immediately called 911, and they took me to the emergency room. For whatever reason, they didn't pump my stomach; they just let me ride it out. I think it made my recovery even more difficult. I don't remember much of that night except going in and out of consciousness.

After a day or two, I was more coherent. They brought in a social worker who dealt with attempted suicides. He asked me the typical questions about why I had tried to take my life and whether I planned to hurt myself again. He suggested I go back to my previous psychiatric facility. I declined because I knew they couldn't help me. He thanked me and left. While he was gone, he got a court order for me to be put back into the psychiatric facility anyway.

Next thing I knew, a bunch of cops were in my hospital room. They told me I had to go to the facility, but I refused. Instantly, there was total chaos. Six police officers were trying to hold me, but because of my workouts, I was pretty strong. That, combined with pure adrenaline, made me unstoppable. They had me on the ground but could not

A Different Kind of Strong

contain me. I was laughing at them. The six of them could not handcuff me.

While I was down on the ground, I could hear my mother crying and begging, "Danny, stop it. Please stop it!" She hated seeing what was happening to me and wanted me to comply. Finally, I took her advice and stopped resisting. They handcuff me and strap me to a gurney.

I was then put in an ambulance and taken back to the mental-health center. At the facility, they put me in a padded room until I became more cooperative. I knew one of the workers there from my last visit. He helped me calm down and get out of that room. I knew that place wouldn't help me, but I did the program again anyway and followed the rules. I was released a week later.

In the previous three years, I had changed so many things in my life. I had stopped drinking, smoking, and doing drugs, and I gave up pornography. I was going to church. I was paying off debt. That was another great burden I couldn't carry all by myself. I had past medical bills of about $20,000. I tried to pay, but it was too much. I would eventually file for bankruptcy.

I still needed help mentally, emotionally, and especially spiritually. My mom called my dad. He and my stepmom had recently moved from California to Washington. We all decided that I should move to Spokane with them, just a couple of hours north of Richland. Maybe I would find peace there.

CHAPTER 6

Mind, Body, Spirit

When I got to Spokane, I willingly went to another psychiatric facility. They wanted to put me on drugs. Fortunately, my body kept rejecting the drugs, and I'm so glad they did. After a week, I was released and did outpatient therapy with a nurse practitioner. I was diagnosed with bipolar disorder. To this day, I don't think that was correct. He put me on lithium. I'm not sure if it ever worked or not.

After about eight months, I stopped taking the prescription because I found out that over time, it could damage my liver. I thought I had done enough to my liver in my drinking days and didn't need anything else to contribute harm.

It took me a year to fully recover after my attempted suicide. I was drained mentally, physically, and emotionally. I could feel that my body was super weak. I kept trying to stay healthy and work out, but I knew I wasn't the same. Over time, though, I got better.

I tried to transfer to another grocery store in Spokane, but it never worked out. I knew I needed a job but wasn't sure what to do. While in Richland, I had worked on a certification to become a personal trainer. I had never planned on it for a career; I was just doing it to improve my health and gain overall knowledge of fitness and nutrition. But now, I studied the material again, completed the certification, and got my first job at a gym.

This was an environment where I felt very confident and comfortable. Things were going OK. But I was still struggling inside. People always perceived me as happy and healthy, but I was really going through hell—literally. I moved out of my dad's and got my own apartment. At this time in my life, I had completely given up on religion. I was angry at God and had stopped going to church. I thought the gospel of Jesus Christ didn't work and that my life was proof of it. I remember throwing all my scriptures and anything to do with religion in a dumpster. I was frustrated and very mad. I couldn't understand why I was going through so much hell when I was trying so hard to change. I just couldn't understand. How was it possible?

I worked on a new certification to become a specialist in performance nutrition. One of the assignments was to ask ten gym members why they thought they were not reaching their fitness goals. Their reasons were astounding: posttraumatic stress disorder (PTSD), bipolar disorder, major depression, lupus, diabetes, physical injuries, and eating addictions.

I will never forget the woman with PTSD. Her husband had killed himself years earlier, and her fourteen-year-old daughter was living on the streets, doing drugs. I remember asking myself, "How am I supposed to motivate these people?" The answer was that I couldn't. I could motivate them for an hour while I trained them, but what about the other twenty-three hours of their days?

I shared what our members had been telling me with the owner of the gym. I asked what we were going to do about it. He said not to worry and that this was just the way it was. He told me that only about 1–2 percent of people actually achieve their gym goals. After that day, our relationship changed. That's when I started to study the mind and find ways of self-empowerment. Little did I know that the search was actually for me. I also decided to start my own personal-training business.

As I worked at the gym and did my business on the side, my relationship with the owner only got worse. He hired someone else to be the training director, and I felt denied and betrayed. The manager had told me that I was going to get the job.

I got involved with a gym employee named Karrie. I liked her a lot. We became close and spent a lot of time together. We watched movies, went for drives, and went out to dinner. She had a little boy whom I adored, and he adored me as well. We played whenever we had the chance. Life seemed to be getting better.

Then something unexpected happened. I began training a young kid of about fourteen who had the potential to become a professional hockey player. His parents and coaches wanted him to gain speed, strength, and muscle. I worked with him on a regular basis, and he was getting excellent results. He was bulking up and getting stronger.

One day while working him out, I had him on a leg-press machine. I was putting on hundred-pound plates, and I rotated my torso while holding one of them. That's when I injured my low back again. I knew something was wrong. I told the kid that something bad had happened, but I continued to train him.

Although I was clearly injured, I tried to work through it while going to physical therapy. I had been paying out of my own pocket until one day, the physical therapist asked me why, since I had gotten hurt on the job. He had a point. I didn't want to create any problems at work, but I could no longer afford to pay and decided to file a claim for workers' compensation.

After the physical setback came another emotional breakdown. Karrie decided to end our relationship. I was ticked off! Why did this keep happening? Why couldn't a relationship with a woman ever work out? I was frustrated and losing hope again.

That's when I made a huge mistake. One weekend night, my back was giving me tremendous pain, and I was trying to find relief. I couldn't locate a massage therapist, so I went to a massage center. They gave me a massage. And then they offered much more. I had not been with a woman for about four and a half years. I was giving up on life again and was very lonely. I gave in. That's when I paid for sex for the first—and the last—time.

I tried not to care about what I had done, but I couldn't. I felt dirty. I also felt I had participated in further ruining a woman's life. I couldn't keep it to myself any longer, so I confided in my dad. I felt better by just talking to him about it. He helped me to understand that I could repent and be forgiven.

Around this time is when I met Sally. She had discontinued her gym membership because she was getting married and moving. But she returned, saying that things hadn't worked out and she wanted her membership back. One day, I walked up to her while she was on the treadmill and said, "I know you don't know me, but you're probably going through a lot. If you need someone to talk to, you can talk to me." She thanked me. I smiled and walked away. She later asked if I could help her train for a half marathon. I agreed.

Because Karrie had rejected me, I stopped interacting with her son. To get even with me, she told the owner I was harassing her. He called me into his office, and we got into a heated argument about a couple of issues. He fired me on the spot. I didn't care. I was done with all of them anyway.

I went back one last time to return my work shirts and get my last paycheck. Sally came up and said she had been looking for me. She still wanted me to train her. I agreed and started to help her prepare for the half marathon. She was a great person. We started spending a lot of time together and ended up dating. However, I remember thinking that something wasn't quite right about the relationship. I even talked to her about it. She started crying and wasn't happy with that news. I gave in, overriding my intuition. I eventually asked her to marry me.

From the outside, our relationship looked amazing. We were both fit and healthy, we got along great, and we had many things in common. We seldom argued. Everyone thought we were the perfect couple. We opened a gym together. It was called Absolute Fitness Empowerment Center. We were going to be partners in marriage and in business. Everything fell together nicely.

In our business, we went about health and fitness differently from traditional gyms. We took a holistic approach. I did my best to combine different techniques I had learned. I wanted to help people be emotionally stable so they could be successful in their eating habits and fitness programs. I wanted them to be empowered and take control of their health and their lives.

At the gym, Sally offered mental and emotional counseling to our clients. We both became certified in a technique that helps people overcome self-sabotaging behaviors. I was the fitness and nutrition expert. We offered massage therapy, yoga, tai chi, and meditation as well. Ours was also known as the gym that helped post-gastric-bypass surgery patients develop a healthier way of living. Things were going well.

But that didn't last. The gym wasn't even open for a year before we ran into financial problems due to the economy, geographical location, and high overhead. Owning a gym is expensive. We had to close. We talked to the landlord, and he let us out of the lease early. That was a miracle. I was thankful for his understanding.

After closing the gym, I met two guys who owned a fitness business. They read the story of my past struggles and all I had overcome on my website. They thought I was the perfect fit to join their team. Eventually, I could be a partner. They were projecting to make $30 million a year. It was a great opportunity. Or so I thought at the time.

Life has its ways of teaching us things. That's exactly what came next: another big lesson. I went for a run with my wife one day. When we got back, I went to the bathroom and remember putting the toilet seat down. Something happened to my back again. A few hours later, I was in the most excruciating pain of my life. I couldn't sit, stand, or lie down for more than a couple of minutes. I could barely walk. The pain was so bad that I thought if I'd been at the edge of a cliff, I would have jumped.

I didn't like prescription drugs, so I didn't want to go to the emergency room. But after being in this horrible situation for three days, I went to the hospital. I couldn't take it anymore. They gave me pain meds and muscle relaxers. The doctors wanted me to have surgery right away, but I chose to go to an orthopedic surgeon whom my cousin (a surgeon himself) recommended. That doctor didn't see the need to do surgery right away; he was the conservative type. So we played it safe. I tried many therapies and different processes to get me back to health. I tried chiropractic treatments, physical therapy, massage therapy, nutrition, meditation, and energy healing, along with emotional and mental therapy techniques. But nothing seemed to work.

Eventually, I agreed to another back surgery. I was in bed for eight months and then had a back-fusion surgery that kept me in bed for another three months. So I was almost completely bedridden for nearly a year. While going through this difficult physical situation, I was struggling even more emotionally. I sunk into depressive states again and spiraled downward.

One day, a friend of my wife's came over and gave me a book. In it, the author said that at one point, he had been very successful in a different industry, yet he knew something was missing in his life, and that left him unhappy. He began a personal journey of self-exploration that took him around the world to meet spiritual masters.

The book was about letting go. I had never studied anything like it before, but it all made sense. I was fascinated by the author's writings and videos. I watched hundreds of talks while lying in bed. I began to have an inner awareness of self.

While I was in bed, home teachers from the LDS church contacted me, and missionaries stopped by periodically. My wife didn't want anything to do with them, and it made things very uncomfortable in our home. I asked my home teacher what it would take for him to stop calling and for the missionaries to stop coming over. He said I would have to remove my name from church records. So I did, having no idea what the consequences of that decision would be.

At that point, Sally and I were involved in the new-age energy-healing community. We were considered Reiki "masters" and were going to a church that welcomed and promoted energy healing. They accepted anything. That sounds great—but God's ways are not our ways.

Every day, Sally and I picked a tarot card and checked our daily astrology. A thought started coming into my mind—I wondered if I was with the right person. Then the thought grew: *Am I even with the right sex?* I started to wonder if I was gay. This was very disturbing to me. My mind started putting a false puzzle together. I liked romantic comedies. I liked to cook. I liked hanging out with women. I liked shopping for clothes. Once in a while, I would see a guy and think he was good-looking. This is something guys never admit because that would mean they're gay, right?

The more I thought of it, the more gay indicators appeared in my life. I noticed more gay people. I drove by a gay bar that I had never seen before. It seemed that what I thought about, I brought about.

One night, I was in great turmoil. I wanted to know if I was gay. I sat with a tarot deck and said, "Just give it to me straight," and I picked a card. It told me yes. *No, please no,* I thought. I mixed the cards and picked again. The same card.

Over the next couple of days, I did it one or two more times. Same card. That put me in a state of actual hell. I pleaded with God. In that moment, I started to go back to my old suicidal thoughts. I would rather die than be gay. I decided to go back to my psychologist. I was not in a good frame of mind.

I struggled for a while and talked to my wife about it. She kind of chuckled and told me I wasn't gay. She couldn't see the workings of Satan, the law of attraction, and my mind playing tricks on me. Thankfully, by the grace of God, I soon came to the conclusion that I was not gay. I caught the lie. When it comes to who we truly are, we are nothing contrary to God.

Months after the surgery, we went to a small concert at a vineyard. I had not touched alcohol for almost eight years but decided I needed a break—a break from myself and my strict lifestyle, really. I had a couple of glasses of wine that night. That led to us drinking wine in our house, then beer, and then hard alcohol. I also frequented several bars. I was trying to find balance in my life between letting loose and being rigid.

One night, I went out with a friend and got very drunk. I had one drink and couldn't feel anything, so I had another and then another. I remembered waking up in my bed the next morning, not sure what had happened. "What am I doing?" I asked myself. What had I been thinking? I stopped drinking right away. Even though the drinking spree only lasted a couple of months, it was not a good decision. I had learned that letting loose was not the answer either.

For eight exhausting years, I tried to find peace and happiness. Every day, I searched. I looked into health, fitness, nutrition, counseling, mind-body therapy, religion, and even energy healers. I searched and I searched till I finally surrendered. I came to the conclusion that the world had no answers for me. That was my rock bottom. That's when I decided to take it to my Heavenly Father.

One day, I was praying and asked God to give me an answer. I told Him I was going to open the Bible and to please tell me what to do. What came next was a great surprise. I opened the New Testament right at the part where Jesus was led out into the wilderness to do a forty-day fast. I said to myself, *You've got to be kidding me.* I closed the book and walked away.

A couple of weeks later, I was still troubled. I had to do something. Even my wife was feeling the same way. I went back into the bedroom, and I prayed again. "Heavenly Father, I need your help. I'm going to open the Bible, and please just tell me what to do." So, guess what page I opened to? It was the same page. That's when I started thinking seriously about it. To be honest, God had been dropping hints before, but I just didn't take them seriously. I mean, think about it. Would you? You would think that's crazy, right? I could die, fasting that long.

I decided to look into it. I talked to some energy healers and asked them if they wanted to do a fast with me. I asked one person who had some land if I could do a fast there. She declined. One of these "spiritual masters" said he would do a two-to-three-day fast out in the wilderness with me. I told him that two or three days wasn't long enough, that I wanted to do a forty-day fast. He didn't think that was a good idea. I explained to him that Jesus, Moses, and Buddha had done it, so why couldn't we? I remember him saying to me, "Yeah, but those were hard-core dudes." In my mind, I believed that besides Jesus, they were just men, just like me. Jesus commands us to be like Him, so why shouldn't we try to be? To make a long story short, nobody wanted to get involved, and I don't blame them. None of them, to this day, know what I have done.

I did a three-day fast at home. I thought maybe that was good enough, but it wasn't. My wife told me that there was still something I had to do. In that moment, I was reminded again of Jesus's forty-day fast. I knew I had to do it, even though I was only eight months postsurgery. The healing time for that type of operation was a year. This may seem like it was bad timing, but change is always inconvenient.

There was a place where my wife and I used to go, a place she loved. It was where we had gone running together when I was training her for the half marathon. We talked about the fast, and we agreed that it was something I needed to do. She suggested that I drink some water while out there. I set a date and prepared myself. I packed up my car with all the stuff I thought I needed: firewood, warm clothes, a tent, a Bible, and a few other things. I was off to the woods.

CHAPTER 7
THE FAST

On October 14, 2011, I went to a state park in Spokane, Washington. I arrived at 11:00 a.m. but had actually started my fast at 9:00 p.m. the night before. I asked for a forty-day pass, but they only allowed up to thirty days. I agreed and paid for that. To be honest with you, I wasn't sure if I was going to do a thirty-, forty-, or fifty-day fast. I just needed to do it as long as it took for me to receive the answers I needed.

The campsite was quiet and gave me a sense of peace. The fresh air was cleansing, filling my lungs with newness. I was surrounded by trees, rocks, and a rushing river. Clouds were in the sky, and it looked like there was possible rain heading my way. Rain or shine, I was not leaving. My campsite location was on a cul-de-sac, far from the ranger's station, which was great. I didn't want anyone to know what I was doing.

The first thing I learned while setting up camp was that the more stuff I had, the more I had to attend to. Wow! Great insight. Isn't it true? The bigger the house, the more rooms there are to clean.

After I set up camp and got everything organized, I walked over to a bench overlooking the Columbia River. I grabbed a stick, and in the dirt, I wrote the word *VICTORY*. As I wrote the final letter, I heard geese flying above me and looked up. They were in a perfect V formation. Victory! I knew it was mine! In that moment, I knew that God and I were going to accomplish what we had set out to do. I needed His help, and that was a sign to me that I was not alone and I was protected. God was with me.

I felt like exploring the area, so I walked to the top of a cliff overlooking the river. What a sight. The view from the immense cliff was spectacular. High above, I gazed over the rapids that flowed through the massive vein that must have taken millions of years to create. Giant boulders along the side of the river could only have been created and placed there by something divine.

As I stood at the top, a strange feeling came over me. What if I fell? What if I jumped? I wasn't planning on jumping; it was just my mind messing with me and the temptation of Satan. Later that day, I read the story of how Satan tempted Jesus to jump off a cliff, promising that angels would catch him. The story also talked about Satan telling Jesus to turn stones into bread to tempt him to eat. I was later tempted in similar ways.

I continued discovering the area. Sometimes I drove, and other times, I walked. There were different campsites throughout the grounds. I found my favorite spots. Another campsite area just south of mine was the place to hang out with the geese. It was right along the riverbed—a perfect location for them to gather. Another one of my favorites was closer to camp. It also ran along the riverbed, but this particular getaway had a beach. There I walked around in the sand, feeling the earth between my toes. I laid out in the sun and enjoyed getting in the water. The river was cold but very invigorating.

There was another location I drove to just north of the site. It had a huge area perfect for a picnic. But this was going to be no picnic, and there surely wasn't going to be anything to eat. As a few days went by, I started feeling the fatigue setting into my body from having no nutrients. I realized that I needed to conserve my energy, so I tried not to move around as much.

One day, a family of deer came walking through my campsite, heading up the hill. They were beautiful and their eyes mesmerizing. I was in such a peaceful state of mind that I started to talk to them. They stopped and looked at me as I told them I was not going to hurt them and that I loved them. I was feeling very calm, and they could tell. After a couple of minutes, I told them good-bye, and they immediately went up the hill—the fawn first and the adults following, in much the same way that shepherds move their flocks.

At night I made a fire to keep warm, and it gave me something to do. It might not seem like a big chore, but in my weakening state, keeping a fire going was taxing. It was worth the effort, though, as the crackling of the fire put my mind at ease, and the dance of the flame was pleasing to my eyes.

One night, I heard what sounded like a dog howling—so I thought. Then I heard another one, and one after that. Then I thought to myself, *I don't think they are dogs. I think they are wolves.* They were all around me in the distance, and I knew it was Satan trying to distract me. He was trying to put fear in me with each howl, trying to create anxiety in my chest. Well, I wasn't going to budge. Nothing was going to stop me. I told myself that I was going to do this even if I died trying. I told Satan to show himself. I told him, "Let's take care of this once and for all." I don't know if it was confidence or stupidity, but I had had enough. He never showed himself, but he was present.

The weather started to get really cold, and the tent wasn't going to suffice anymore. Plus, getting in and out of the tent and sleeping on the hard ground were giving me back problems. I was in a lot of pain because I was still recovering from a major back surgery. I called my wife, and she came to switch cars with me. She owned an SUV with back seats that folded down, so I could sleep in it. This was certainly a lot better than the tent. I needed to stay warm and comfortable for the sake of my back, so staying in the car was a much better idea.

Inside the car, I read a lot. I read the Bible and also listened to a lot of talks about letting go. One talk in particular stood out. It was about a person who had many different rooms in which to do things. He eventually got bored with all the stuff he had. One day, he found a room he had never seen before. In it was a tall object underneath a blanket. When he pulled the blanket off, he saw that it was a mirror. Standing in front of it, he stared at his own reflection. He was being shown himself. This is exactly what was happening to me during my experience.

Satan kept trying to tear me down and wear me down. He tried to tempt me in little, subtle ways. The constant thought of food consumed me. Sitting on a bench near a patch of grass where the geese met, I was tempted. Satan tempted me, "Just eat one little blade of grass." I knew the thought was coming from him. I was not going to give in. Even though it looked good, that one blade of grass could have negated the whole thing. I recalled Satan tempting the Savior by challenging Him to turn stones into bread. That was a great lesson for me. It showed me how surrendering to even such a small temptation can ruin something great.

I had several dreams out there, which was another way Satan tried to distract me. In the first dream, I was fighting an enormous snake. The battle was on the edge of a cliff, with me precariously positioned at the edge. Fire in the distance symbolized the depths of hell. We battled back and forth, and then the snake became vulnerable enough for me to strike it with a deadly roundhouse kick to the head. The snake went down. But it soon emerged again in my next dream.

In it, the snake wasn't as big, but it was just as dangerous. To end this particular battle, I needed to sever its head. I was given a sword. I'd never learned how to use one, but in my dream, I was a master. The snake came in to strike several times as I maneuvered out of harm's way. Once again the snake became exposed, and I went in for the kill. With one smooth, powerful strike, I took the snake's head clean off. Even though the head was removed, that didn't mean that Satan was done. He always wants us to think that he is gone, but he is immortal and extremely committed to his destructive plan.

In another dream, Satan tempted me with a naked woman who told me I could have her if I sold my soul. Without hesitation, I looked firmly into her eyes and said that my soul belonged to God and God only. She became sad and tried to lure me in with guilt, but it didn't work. I was immovable in my faith.

Next came a dream of a road that led straight up into the sky. I saw people who seemed to be from other planets. They were in UFO-like ships, being transported to Heaven. I wanted to go with them, but it was not my time.

Recalling all these dreams, I realize that they were symbolic and very significant. They taught me who I truly am—a valiant warrior of truth and light. They showed me that if I used the tools given (the sword or word of God), I could overcome the powers of hell. They also helped me to understand that if I stayed true, I would be transported to heaven too and be exalted on high. They are dreams I will never forget.

One day, I was lying in the car, and the cleansing became intense. I was going through the repentance process and releasing painful tears. I cried off and on for several days as my life flashed before my eyes. Everything I had ever done was displayed on a mental screen. All the mistakes I had made. All the people I had hurt. I saw how I had negatively affected so many lives, including my own. I felt the pains of my sin. Like Alma the younger, I was experiencing a racked and tormented soul, and I'm so glad I did. That was the moment when my conversion took place.

Heavenly Father is so loving. In my deepest moment of despair, hope came. I heard something going on outside the car. I sat up and looked out of the window, and to my astonishment, hundreds of doves were on the ground, encircling my vehicle. The doves were nowhere else in the entire campground. I was overcome with a sense of peace. Tears continued to flow down my face like the river in the distance, but this time, it was not out of regret but because of His love for me. I was experiencing a wonderful process of cleansing, healing, and forgiveness that only God can provide.

It says in the New Testament that a dove came down and fell upon Jesus after He was baptized. The dove symbolized the Holy Ghost, the great Comforter. I knew once again in that moment that I was not alone. I felt the comfort sent to me by God, my Heavenly Father.

I often took drives in the area to occupy my time. It helped me to get away from camp and feel the cool wind in my face. I would also leave the car running at night so I could use the heater to keep warm. Between driving and keeping

A Different Kind of Strong

the car running, I eventually used up my gas, so I had to fill up. Luckily, there was a store about a mile up the road.

It was odd being in "the world" again, but I just kept quiet and did what I had to do. I didn't want any distractions. I bought a sports drink, gassed up the car, and put air in the tires. Then I walked out to the parking lot, opened the bottle, and poured it out. Back to the campsite I went with my empty bottle.

Almost three weeks into the fast, I grew weary. The bathroom was only about a hundred feet from my campsite, but I had been driving to it quite often because I was so exhausted. Eventually, even that became tough. Then I had started relieving myself outside of the car, but then that became a problem too. Just getting out of the car became a major task. That's where the empty sports drink bottle came in. I now had my own urinal in the car.

Even taking a shower in the restrooms and brushing my teeth became very taxing. Taking clothes off and putting them back on was a draining chore. Every movement was a challenge. So hygiene became less important. Besides, who was going to smell me anyway?

Several times during my fast, I felt great anxiety. I felt extremely uncomfortable and wanted to crawl out of my skin. I dealt with it by being still and not moving. I would "sit in it," feel it, and experience it. These were strengths I had learned from the techniques of letting go. The world believes that the way to deal with problems is to do something, to distract our minds from the disturbance. When we do that, we never face the real issue. Uncomfortable feelings and fear make us want to run toward something. It demands our attention and then pushes us around like a bully. I was not going to be pushed around anymore, so I sat in it. It was very painful at times, but it was a great lesson. As the Lord says, "Be still. This too shall pass."

Throughout the fast, I had a strong, repeated impression saying, "Come back to Me." Once in a while, I called my dad on the phone just to talk. He thought I was just camping. I told him I wanted to go back to church—in other words, I wanted to come back to Him (God). This was very symbolic. I had gone to the wilderness to be with my Heavenly Father, and I increased my communication with my earthly father. I poured out my heart to both of them. I wanted to come "home," meaning that I wanted to go back to church. I was receiving an answer to the question, "What do I do?"

On day thirty, I was deeply feeling the effects of the fast. I was very tired and felt like I was fading quickly. I prayed and pleaded with Heavenly Father to help me and to give me the strength to keep going. At about eight thirty that night, I asked my Heavenly Father, with tears running down my face, "Are we done yet? Can I go home now, please?" After a long plea, I opened up the Bible to a page, and in one of the verses were the words *go home*. I was finally being released.

I had done all that I needed to do. I had gone through the repentance process and had a true change of heart. After finding out what to do, I knew I needed to go back to church.

I knew then that we were done with the fast. I was so happy. I was praising God. I was so excited to go home!

Suddenly, I had energy. I was able to pack up the car, no longer feeling the effects of the fast. I'm not sure if it was adrenaline or sheer excitement, but I had the strength to move. I prayed and thanked God. That was where I experienced His mercy. I yelled from the top of my lungs, "Hallelujah!" as I was packing up the car. I yelled it out the window as I drove home. I was going "home!"

My total fast had been for thirty days. I met three things out there: good (feeling God's love and mercy), evil (temptation like never before), and myself (the natural man). The scariest thing was seeing myself. After seeing all the consequences of my actions, I had a change of heart. I never wanted to hurt anyone or anything ever again. This experience had completely changed my life. I was never the same.

When I got home, no one was there. My wife had gone on a retreat and would be back in a couple of days. I started juicing fruits and vegetables. I didn't want to rush my eating, but I couldn't help it. I was so hungry. Shortly, my body went into shock, and I threw up all I had eaten. I ate again and then threw it all back up. My body eventually remembered how to digest food but not without pain. I had cramping below my stomach for weeks. Trying to readjust to normal eating habits was extremely difficult.

I remember thinking how different "the world" looked when I first went back to it. But in time, I came to understand that the world wasn't different—I was. I saw how much my attitude and language had changed, and I started to dress more respectably. And, as I mentioned, I felt like I never ever wanted to hurt anyone or anything ever again.

After dedicating myself to that fast, I thought Heavenly Father was going to fix everything in my life. That's exactly what He did—but not in the way I thought He would. As I mentioned, during the fast, I was prompted to go back to the LDS church. I had felt that way even before the fast. I knew it was the Lord's true church, and it was where He wanted me to be.

My wife wanted nothing to do with the church, so my choice made our relationship difficult. We tried to hold on to our marriage, but we knew something was wrong. There was, as they say, an elephant in the room. That elephant was the lack of the gospel of Jesus Christ and the influence of the Holy Spirit in our home.

I thought I might have another back surgery, and Sally said she didn't know if she could go through that again. I didn't blame her. But her saying so made it easier for me to consider leaving. She was a very good woman and had helped me a lot, but we just were not meant to be. Were we truly in love? Was it "true love" that we had? I don't think so. I don't think we knew what that meant.

We separated, and I went to live with my dad. I took my clothes and personal belongings, and nothing else. Stuff didn't seem to matter to me anymore. Everything I owned fit underneath a bed at my dad's house.

I had just lost my wife, my stepson, my dog, my home, my business, my health, my career, and many intangible things like confidence and self-esteem. I had given up my church membership, the priesthood, and all the blessings that came with that. This was definitely my "Job experience" (Referring to Job, a prophet in the Holy Bible). I had literally lost everything. But my fast had helped me discover that I had to lose everything in order to gain it all. Luke 9:24 states, "For whosoever will save his life must be willing to lose it for my sake; and whosoever will be willing to lose his life for my sake, the same shall save it."

- Embraces pain during fast; comes out well!
- Leaves current wife

CHAPTER 8

The Comeback

I WENT BACK TO CHURCH for the first time with my dad. I have to admit that I was angry. After all I had done to change, why was all the negative stuff happening? Why wasn't my wife sitting next to me in church? Why wouldn't the Lord help me bring her with me? Even though it was hard to be there, I stuck with it.

Each week, it got better as my focus turned to service. I became the missionary taxi. I would visit members and do home teaching. I went to all church functions. I would even go to the temple with my dad once a week and meditate in the waiting room while he did an endowment session. Just because you don't have a temple recommend doesn't mean you can't go to the temple and feel the spirit.

I scheduled weekly meetings with my bishop. In our first meeting, I told him that I was not there to make friends or go on dates. I was there to come closer to God. I needed to make things right with my Heavenly Father. I was serious this time.

Because I had removed my name from church records, my bishop suggested that I take the missionary lessons. Brilliant idea. I needed to start all over. The amazing thing was that I began to understand the scriptures like never before. I just got it. Line upon line, precept upon precept, I learned the fundamentals of the gospel, and it all made sense.

One day, a thought came to me while I was reflecting on my situation: "Remember when you said that anybody can be happy in any situation? Now is your chance to prove that point." I remembered saying this years earlier. The Lord was challenging me to prove a statement I had made long ago to see if it was true. This was the perfect setting for me to find out. Like I said, I had lost everything. While I was in my dad's room, watching TV, I made a choice. The choice was to be happy. Yes, happiness is a choice. I was going to be happy no matter what.

I was in a state of happiness for a couple of months. I was fully content. Nothing could get to me, and nothing could stir me up to frustration or anger. It was unbelievable. How could this be? How could somebody who had lost everything be so happy and content? One of the reasons was that I had chosen to be. What power it is that we are given! We have the power to be happy, and we have the power to be sad. It is our choice and nobody else's. Nobody can make us be either one. We decide which to be.

The other reason was that I was not sinning. Some say, "Live the commandments, and you'll be happy." This is true. I made a regretted decision that took all that happiness away from me: I partook in the selfish act of self-gratification. This is a transgression against sexual purity. This behavior was something I had struggled with ever since I was a kid. I was upset and angry with myself and fell into a depressive state. I noticed that when I sinned, it affected my spirit and state of mind. Because I did something that was contrary to my Heavenly Father, happiness went away. Happiness is a choice, but if we do not live a choice life, happiness cannot remain.

    Even though my months of happiness came to an end, I'm grateful that they did. This taught me that keeping the commandments really does bring happiness. When we don't, we become depressed, feeling regret, sorrow, and shame. I also learned that if I stayed in this state of contentment, I wouldn't want or need anything. But there were many things I needed in order to return to my Heavenly Father: repentance, membership, eternal marriage, and covenants needed to be restored, and this took effort. Once I realized these truths, I overcame the addiction to self-gratification once and for all. It was the last addiction for me to conquer.

    It was time to start dating again, so I went to activities for singles. Friends of the family tried setting me up with their daughter. My dad thought it might be a good idea too. She was young and liked me a lot. She visited, but I just didn't feel comfortable. I wasn't able to be myself around her. She was very beautiful but not for me.

    After spending time with this girl, I heard something. I'm not sure where it came from, but this is what I heard: "Your

A Different Kind of Strong

earthly parents are not the ones who are going to choose your eternal companion. Your heavenly parents are." (Yes, we have a Heavenly Mother.) It was plain as day. It was a direct message from my Heavenly Father.

I dated a little bit in Spokane, but nothing seemed to really work out. Either I really liked a woman and she didn't like me, or it was the other way around. It was frustrating and too familiar.

I had played guitar off and on since I was twelve years old but never got really serious about it. After the fast and once I returned to the gospel and understood its importance, I started writing songs about Heavenly Father, the gospel of Jesus Christ, and my life experiences. I wrote songs every week. Next thing I knew, I had written nearly twenty of them. They came almost effortlessly through inspiration.

While watching the BYU channel one day, I saw a show about music. It was like my Heavenly Father was talking to me. I felt He was telling me to pursue music. I also felt prompted to move. Spokane was no longer serving me, and I was done serving it. It was time for me to move on.

I thought again about Southern California where I had grown up. I thought of sunny weather and the beach. That sounds great, right? Then I heard the words *Salt Lake*. I said to myself, *But it snows, and it's cold over there. I've had enough of that here in Washington.* I reminded myself that I had always done things my way—and this time, I was going to trust the Lord.

I told my dad and my brother of my plans. I don't think they really believed me at first. But whether they did or not, it didn't matter. It was where the Lord wanted me, and that's where I was going. We had a farewell party with family and friends from church. I was going to Salt Lake City to spread the gospel through music. I had a mini concert in my dad's living room the night before I started on my new adventure and life. That's exactly what I wanted. I wanted everything new.

My dad tried to give me things to take there: dishes, silverware, and kitchen items. I didn't want them. I didn't want anything from anybody. This was something the Lord and I were going to do together. I wanted a new life, and that meant everything new: furniture, silverware, dishes, and a new bed. I wanted a totally new life, and that's exactly what I was about to get.

The day had come. It was Halloween—October 31, 2013. I knew that my family did not want to see me go, but I knew I had to move on with my life and start over. It was the perfect time.

While I drove to Utah, the Adversary's fiery darts of doubt penetrated my mind. I was overcome with fear. I knew no one in Salt Lake. I had no place to live. The chattering mind started to lay into me. "You can't do it. What do you think you're doing? You're going to fail." Satan was working on me. He didn't want me to do what I was about to do. I just prayed and put my foot on the gas. It was one of the best decisions I ever made.

I knew that I had to do what the Lord was asking me to do. I felt like the ancient prophet Nephi, who said, "I will go and do the things which the Lord hath commanded, for I know that the Lord giveth no commandments unto the children of men, save he shall prepare a way for them that they may accomplish the thing which he commandeth them" (1 Nephi 3:7).

- Satan keeps chattering in his ear
- God tells him to move to Salt Lake City.

CHAPTER 9

A NEW LIFE

———

WHEN I ARRIVED IN SALT Lake, the first thing I did was go straight to LDS Business College. I had been wanting to go back to school for quite some time, and this one seemed a perfect fit. I pulled off the freeway and took a tour of the campus. I felt peace and comfort. This was the place I needed to be, for sure. I was still on workers' compensation for my back injury and didn't know if they would approve me going back to school. But before leaving Spokane, I knew Heavenly Father would help me no matter what happened.

For the first couple of nights, I stayed with a cousin who lived in a nearby town, but I found an apartment downtown right away, exactly where I wanted to be. I hit it off with the landlord, and he approved me on the spot. I had my apartment. Now, all I had to do was fill it up. Then my wish came true: new furniture, silverware, dishes, and a new bed! I had a whole new home.

Music and the Spoken Word is a televised, spiritual musical performance by the Mormon Tabernacle Choir, and I started attending it every Sunday before church. As a newcomer in town, I toured the Temple Square grounds often. I called it "Mormon Disneyland." I felt right at home.

I started developing a social life. I began attending a midsingle adult ward and went on a few dates. I also thought about my music and what I was going to do with it. How would I begin, and where would I perform? I purchased new sound equipment in preparation. This was a new adventure, and I loved it!

On November 17, 2013, I went to *Music and the Spoken Word*. I sat up front, as usual, and noticed a beautiful woman. She asked if the seat next to me was taken. I told her it wasn't and smiled. Not only was she beautiful, but she was also a missionary. Her name was Sister Binkhurst. She wasn't a twenty-something but more my age. We talked a little bit about where I was from and what I was doing in Salt Lake City.

After the broadcast, she gave me a card with her e-mail address on it and asked how she could be of service. I wasn't quite sure. I asked her if she wanted to go to a singles dance, not really understanding the rules of her mission. She was a full-time missionary but didn't seem to have a companion. She politely said that she couldn't but shared that the stand-up bass player in the orchestra had her eye on me. I had been completely unaware of that and thanked her for offering to help me. We parted ways, but I continued to think about her.

Two weeks later, I followed Sister Binkhurst's hunch and asked the stand-up bassist out on a date. She accepted, and we went to dinner. One day, she invited me to go to the Mormon Tabernacle Christmas party with her. I was completely blown away. I went from knowing nobody to attending one of the best Christmas parties in Salt Lake! All these great things were happening so quickly, and I was loving it.

I e-mailed Sister Binkhurst a few days after we met, even though I had really wanted to reach out to her the next day. I discovered that she served in the Family History Department. I wanted to do genealogy work for my family, so I contacted her, and we worked on my family history. We started going to the temple and helping each other. We got to know each other a little more. I told her about my health and fitness background, and she suggested that I meet one of her friends who was interested in health and nutrition.

At the temple, I was introduced to Audrey. She was like Sister Binkhurst's unofficial companion. They were both very special and gospel oriented. It seemed like all they wanted to do was help people and bring them to Christ. They were true missionaries. From that day forward, we became the three Musketeers. We did many things together: go to the temple, go out to eat, and have deep gospel discussions.

Sister Binkhurst became my personal missionary. She started to teach me and helped me discover things I never knew I needed. She e-mailed me information and gave me study packets. They were all gospel-based principles and exactly what I needed. She had a message for me one day and said it was from Heavenly Father. She said she had delayed giving it to me because it was awkward. A part of the

A Different Kind of Strong

message was this: "Have joy, my son!" When I read it, tears came running down my face as I was overcome with emotion. I felt so much of His love for me. For years, I had just wanted Heavenly Father to let me know that He was pleased with me. In that moment, I could feel that He was and that He loved me very much.

I have discovered that He didn't love me because of all the things I went through and overcame. He didn't love me because I chose to follow Him. He loved me because I was His son. He loves all of His children, and He had always loved me.

I had questions for the sister about the message, so I called and asked if we could meet. She said we had to be in a public place. I agreed. One of the mission rules is that a man is not supposed to be alone with a single sister missionary. We were doing our best to respect the Lord.

We met on one of the upper floors of the Joseph Smith Memorial Building. She had some things to talk about too, and so I insisted that she speak first. She told me she had wondered if I was her eternal companion but had come to the conclusion that I was not. That wasn't what I wanted to hear; it hurt a lot. I told her I wanted to run, erase her phone number, and never see her again. This type of cycle had happened over and over again in my life. I tried to keep calm.

The sister had shared some personal things about herself, and so it was my turn. I started to tell her the things I needed to say. I laid it all out, my whole life story. I told her about all the things I used to do, the kind of person I had been, all the trials I had gone through, and the things I had had to overcome. I told her everything. I felt very vulnerable. While I told her these things, I started to shake. My body ached, especially my neck. I felt very uncomfortable. With all that going on, I still stuck with it, telling my whole story.

After we said what we needed to, we parted, thinking we probably weren't the right fit, but she still offered to be my missionary and friend. She was willing to share the things that Heavenly Father was telling her to help me with. One of those things was to teach me what true friendship was all about. That's what made me so uncomfortable. She had put me in the "friend zone." Men can't stand that. It's the worst place possible! The myth is that once you are put in the friend zone, you can never get out.

One day Audrey, Sister Binkhurst, and I spent an afternoon together. We had lunch at the Lion House on Temple Square and had a great conversation. We talked about things that really matter. It was snowing, and as we went outside, Sister Binkhurst's hood got caught in her backpack. I offered to help her. It was as if time stood still when I put her hood on. For some reason, and just for a moment, I felt she was my girlfriend. But she was a missionary and still somewhat a stranger. I didn't even know her that well. Yet it was a strong feeling I had.

Later, we went to the lobby of the Plaza Hotel, right next to Temple Square. Sister Binkhurst had something to discuss with me. One of the things she declared was that we had passed the test of friendship. That was hard to hear. I didn't want to be just friends. I wanted more than that. But I came to accept it. I knew that under normal circumstances, I would have run away. But not this time. I was going to break the cycle! I also couldn't imagine never talking to her again. How could this be? I didn't know her very well, and yet I could not visualize my life without her. In the past, when a relationship didn't work out or someone was not interested, I did my best to just drop it, move forward, and forget about it. But this time, I couldn't. Not with her.

At the Plaza, we got into a deep discussion. I talked about my back injury. I told her that someday, I might be in a wheelchair. She looked me straight in the eye, totally serious, and said in a small, beautiful voice, "I'll push you."

I looked into her eyes and asked her, "Why are you doing this?" I wanted to know why she was helping me.

She said, "Because Heavenly Father and the Lord love you very much."

A feeling came over me that I had never felt before. It was a little uncomfortable and new. I asked her what was going on. "I don't understand what's going on. Something's happening." I said.

She said, "This is something that the world knows nothing about. This is Christlike love." She said this was what Heavenly Father wanted her to teach me. I was totally overwhelmed! It was an enlightening moment. I began to tear up.

It was getting late, and she had to go home. I walked her to the corner and headed to my house. I didn't sleep much that night. Many thoughts went through my mind. Were we going to be together? Should I just walk away? I didn't want to get hurt again. I was already feeling some pain, but I made a decision to see it through. Even if we were just going to be friends, I was not going to run away this time.

I had a dream that night. It was a picture of Sister Binkhurst with another man. He was a very tall man with no real expression on his face. Next to them, but at a distance, were two young boys. After that, I came to terms with the idea that we were never going to be together.

The next day, I told her that I was in turmoil. The best way I could think of to resolve it was to go to the temple and serve others. I asked if she had any temple work for me to do, and she did. After spending several hours there, I was emotionally exhausted, physically drained, hurting, and tired.

Instead of running away, like I usually did, I ended up serving her. Instead of being mad, I went to the temple and humbled myself. The odd part was that I did it all unselfishly. I didn't think I was going to receive a single thing from it. I just did it because it felt like the right thing to do. If she was going to be my true friend, then I was going to be there for her. After that day, things settled down a bit. I got some rest and was able to start thinking straight again. We continued to be friends: Sister Binkhurst, Audrey, and I.

During that time, another wonderful thing happened. One day, I was rushing out the door and locked my keys inside the house. I tried to open the door but couldn't get in. I tried other ways, like through a window, but everything was

A Different Kind of Strong

locked. I tried to call my landlord, but I couldn't reach him. Nothing worked.

It was getting dark and cold, and I was starting to worry a little bit, wondering what to do. I went back down the stairs to try to open the door. It was locked, obviously. As I walked back up the stairs again, I heard a still, small voice say, "Did you think to pray?" Immediately, I stopped in the middle of the staircase and prayed.

I asked Heavenly Father to somehow help me solve this problem and get me into the house. As soon as I was done with the prayer, the voice came back and said, "Go open the door." For a split second, I questioned the voice, but then immediately, my faith overrode my doubt. I walked to the door, grabbed the doorknob, and pushed. I stood there in awe as the door swung open in slow motion. What had just happened? How was this possible? That door had been locked. I knew it was. I had tried to open it many times. I checked the doorknob again. It was still locked.

How did this happen? Now I know. It happened because of the power of prayer. It happened because I had the faith to do what He wanted me to do. It happened because God is all-powerful and can do anything.

Christmas was right around the corner. I had two gifts to give. To Audrey, I gave a book about natural medicine and supplements. It was perfect because she was studying natural medicine. The other gift was a book for Sister Binkhurst: a Book of Mormon study guide. She appreciated my thoughtfulness. The gift had so much meaning and was a treasure to her. I think they both loved their gifts.

On another occasion, we went to the downtown mall to do some shopping. We went to a department store because I wanted to buy some cologne. Sister Binkhurst was looking for a special box to give as a gift to someone. The box she chose was one I pointed out. I didn't know whom the box was for or why she wanted it, but she really liked it. Because I had bought the cologne, the store gave us this beautiful red box for free.

By then, we had all known each other for a few weeks. I invited my friends over for dinner for family-home evening. I told them I could cook them whatever they wanted. They were surprised. I made vegetable korma, and they loved it. They brought some food over as well. We had kind of a potluck between the three of us.

That night, they brought me a gift. Sister Binkhurst told me that Heavenly Father had told her to give it to me. It was the beautiful red box, the one I had picked out for her. Inside its top was the word BELIEVE. In the box were straw, chocolate coins, an instruction card, and many strips of paper—dark yellow and light yellow. This was the instruction card:

A Treasure Chest for Your Righteous Desires
On each strip of light-yellow paper provided, write down something that someone can do to help you feel appreciated, loved, and happy.

A Different Kind of Strong

> On each strip of dark yellow paper provided, write down something that someone has done to help you feel appreciated, loved, and happy.
>
> We aren't born with an instruction manual called *How to Love Me and Help Me Feel Secure, Appreciated, and Loved*. Perhaps by doing these simple things, as you become aware of what it is that creates happy feelings, you will be able to express to others what actions are most meaningful to you, and that will bring you closer to joy.

This was no ordinary gift. This was a gift from my Heavenly Father, not Sister Binkhurst. This was a gift that two loving sisters had taken time and effort to make. This gift was all for me. I was overwhelmed. Tears rolled down my face. I had to turn away because I didn't want them to see me cry, but I couldn't help it. I had never felt so loved in my life.

I told them I had never had friends like them before—friends who didn't want anything from me and who were such a positive influence, friends who just wanted to be friends with me, friends who truly cared about my well-being. I couldn't believe there were people as kind and loving as these two were.

<u>The night they were preparing this gift box for me, I was lying in bed, asking my Heavenly Father a serious question. I wanted to know if Sister Binkhurst and I were going to be together.</u> Was she the one I was supposed to be with? Was she

the one for me? I had never received an answer the way I did when I asked this question. It's called the "burning in the bosom." It was like my whole heart exploded and confirmed that she was the one for me. I carried this overpowering feeling of warmth in my chest for two whole days.

I called the sisters and tried to explain the sensation I was experiencing. They thought I could feel the love they were putting into making the gift for me, but they didn't know about the question I had asked. I knew that Sister Binkhurst was the one and that our Heavenly Father had sent her here for me. But I also knew that she still had to use her agency to want and accept me as her eternal companion.

- Starts getting into music
- Falls in "Christ Like" love with Sister Binkhurst

CHAPTER 10

HONESTY, FRIENDSHIP, AND LOVE

CHRISTMAS CAME, AND I WAS at home by myself. But I was not sad. How could I be? A lot of great things were happening in my life. It was the best Christmas I had ever had. I sent a text to Sister Binkhurst and wished her a merry Christmas. She asked me if I wanted to talk, but she was at a friend's house, so I told her I didn't want to interrupt. She said it was not a problem, so we had a nice phone conversation.

Sister Binkhurst and I met again in the temple. We were sitting in a hallway, talking, and that was when something fascinating happened. She said she saw me age right in front of her. She saw a glimpse of me growing old. She felt that we were going to be friends for a long time.

In the middle of another phone conversation, out of nowhere, I told her that there was only one thing I wanted to do with her. She asked if I was going to tell her what it was. I simply said, "Everything." There was a long pause. Then I reiterated, "I want to do everything—with you." With that one simple word, I had pierced her heart, and she let me in. No one had ever been able to do this to her. She broke down and cried. It was a beautiful moment. Finally, Sister Binkhurst began to have feelings for me too.

Now it all made sense. I found out how she had come to sit next to me that fateful morning at *Music and the Spoken Word*. Her friends Bob and Marla were visiting from California and were with her at the performance. They had been trying to sit together up front. One couple sitting in the front row had plenty of room to scoot over on the bench, but they wouldn't move. I'm so glad that they didn't!

The sister's friends were a little frustrated because they had found room for only two people, but Sister Binkhurst told Bob and Marla that she would find another place for herself. The concert was about to begin, so she prayed to Heavenly Father to know where to sit. She was prompted by a voice that said, "Sit over there, next to him." *I don't want to sit next to him*, she thought. The voice came back, saying, "Talk to him. Be nice."

She answered internally, *I am nice*. Like a good missionary, she followed instructions. And that's really why she sat next to me.

When God brought us together, it was under unusual circumstances. We had been honest and open about uncomfortable matters. As we helped each other, we learned more about each other, and we became real friends. We respected each other and especially the unique situation.

We developed a Christlike love, and that was when we were ready to receive each other and fall in love. She was not some random person I had run into. She was my one and only true love, and I was hers. It was hard for us to believe it was happening, but it was.

When the nature of our friendship changed, Sister Binkhurst went to her mission leader the next day. He asked me to come to his office. I didn't know exactly why, but I agreed to meet him. We talked about what our relationship had become. I told him that we were to be married. It was Heavenly Father's will.

He asked if she wanted to be released early from her mission so we could get married sooner. That was not an option. She had come to serve an eighteen-month mission, and she needed to finish it. I told him that I wanted to do whatever he asked, even if I had to move halfway around the world. He said that wasn't necessary. He also knew that because we were living in the same area, we might run into each other. He explained if that happened, we could greet one another, but then we should part ways. After the meeting, Sister Binkhurst was called into the room, and we discussed all that we had talked about. We both agreed to the conditions that were presented.

She walked me to the elevator and said good-bye as the doors closed. You would think I might have been a little upset or sad about being separated, but I had faith. If this was the way it had to be, then I would wait for her. Seven months remained until the end of her mission.

mmm... We'll see :)

I went to the temple right after that meeting. I found a scripture that helped me know that Heavenly Father was pleased with me. 1 Nephi 3:6 in the Book of Mormon reads, "Therefore go, my son, and thou shalt be favored of the Lord, because thou hast not murmured."

Although we were going to be apart, Sister Binkhurst's mission leaders allowed us to write one e-mail letter per week. It was a great opportunity for us to get to know each other at a distance and a blessing for us, because we could've jumped into things too quickly.

After a couple of letters, I knew I wanted to propose to her. I felt we needed to be married as soon as she completed her mission. I prayed to Heavenly Father for help. My prayer was, "Please, Father, I don't want to propose to her in an e-mail. If it is possible and it is Thy will, put her in front of me."

That evening, I went to the temple with my ward. Waiting for the session to begin, I closed my eyes to meditate and ponder, and when I opened them, I saw a certain someone sitting in front of me. "Is that really her?" I asked myself. I couldn't believe it! I knew it was, but I was amazed. Heavenly Father had heard my prayer and quickly answered it. She had wanted to go to a later session that night instead but was prompted by the Spirit to do an earlier one. We had no idea either one of us was going to be there.

My golden opportunity had come. But it was very awkward. After the session, we were sitting in the Celestial Room. I caught her eye from across the room and hinted to her that we should go upstairs to another room. She shook her head no. What a good, faithful missionary! That's why I loved her so much. She had sold everything she had to go on her mission and serve the Lord. That's the type of woman I wanted to marry and be with for eternity. Through my body language and facial expressions, I tried to imply that my request was OK, but she remained obedient to the Lord.

I went to the sealing room upstairs, hoping she would come. She never did. As I went back down to the other room, I saw her leaving. In my mind, I said, "Oh, no, you don't." I caught up to her at the drinking fountain. I told her it was OK for us to talk, that Heavenly Father was answering my prayer. I told her I had prayed to see her.

As we started downstairs, I stopped her. I looked deep into her eyes and asked if she would marry me. It took her a little while to answer. She had to walk away and think. She said she had to ask herself if she loved me, if she *really* loved me. She asked her spirit and her heart if they loved me. She pictured a lotus flower opening up, and inside was her heart. Her heart was saying yes. She wanted to make sure, so she asked again, and her heart said, "Yes, we love him!"

After she received this confirmation, her answer to me was yes. I was so happy! She was too. It's not every day that a missionary is proposed to inside a temple. I knew that our Heavenly Father had granted me that opportunity, and He wanted it to be special for both of us.

I had already reserved a date and time for us to be sealed in the temple of her choice: the one in Los Angeles. It wasn't because I was that confident in myself; it was because I knew that Heavenly Father wanted us to be together, and I knew she would say yes. There had been no doubt in my mind. This was faith.

Another confirmation that helped us understand that we were meant for each other was that she had wanted to do a forty-day fast at the same time I was out in the wilderness. However, her bishop had helped her understand it was not necessary. What were the chances of two people having that same desire at once?

The next seven months were a challenge. We e-mailed every week and occasionally ran into each other. It was great to see her and know she was OK. She was given permission to go to special events that helped build our faith and relationship. Audrey became the sister's chaperone. They were able to watch me bless the sacrament for the first time, baptize two of my cousin's kids, and attend a friend's sealing in the Salt Lake Temple. We were thankful for her leaders' trust in allowing us to do these things.

While she continued her mission, I tried to save money for the wedding. I didn't have much. I was on a very tight budget. I did my best to save what I could because she was worth it. I wanted to give her everything. Whatever I had, even though it was very little, she could have it all. That's how much I loved her.

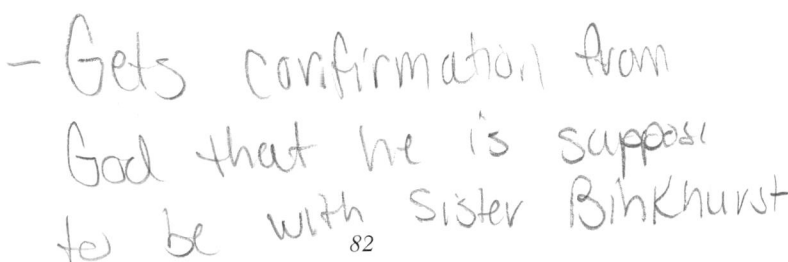

- Gets confirmation from God that he is supposed to be with Sister Birkhurst

CHAPTER 11

Surpassing Expectations

~~~

Through workers' compensation, I was able to go back to school for retraining. It had been a long time since I had been a full-time student. I knew it was going to take a lot of work and effort. I started preparing myself by getting up at 6:00 a.m. and put myself on a schedule as if I were already attending the college.

I took computer classes at a local recreation center and the public library just to get a jump on school. I studied pre-algebra on the web. I also went online and learned about computer programming, which was the degree I was pursuing. I went to the temple to ask Heavenly Father for greater intelligence. As I put forth effort, my mind began to comprehend more of what I was learning. I was preparing myself the best way I could.

Heavenly Father's timing was amazing! Miraculous things happened as admission deadlines were met. Full support from my lawyer, vocational counselor, and school administrators enabled me to enroll quickly and just in time.

But the day my schooling was approved was a day I would be tested. As I cleaned my toilet, something happened to my back again. What's the deal with me and toilets? The last time something like this had happened, I was in bed for eleven months. I couldn't believe it. For a little while, I thought it was because I wasn't supposed to go back to school. Maybe I was being warned that this was not the right path. I found out it was just a test, another test I passed. My back eventually got better, and I started school.

I have to admit, those first few weeks were extremely difficult. I felt like an idiot who didn't know anything about technology. I felt I didn't belong, that I was the most unintelligent person at the school. The majority of students had come right out of high school; they were still in the flow of learning and had grown up using computers. They were able to retain information better than I could. I began to think that school was not for me.

When I had to take my first midterm exam, I froze. I had no idea what to do. I totally forgot everything and couldn't even understand the questions. Everybody else finished the test and left the classroom. The silence was haunting. I couldn't help it. I became very emotional. Tears ran down my face as I talked with my teacher. I told her I didn't know if I could do this. I told her I felt like an idiot. I shared some of my history with her and said that maybe there was something wrong with me. Maybe I had done too much damage to my brain in my partying years. I also felt the consequences of not taking school seriously enough in the past.

My teacher stayed with me until I calmed down. She helped me gain confidence in myself and told me to not give up. She mentioned other resources at the school for students who struggled with learning. I also prayed to Heavenly Father for help and had faith that it would come. Help came.

Whenever things got tough, I prayed, took a deep breath, and pulled out Sister Binkhurst's picture on my phone. That was all I needed to do. As long as I focused on God and why my education was important, I got through it. I told myself to just focus on one assignment at a time and get back to work. These practices kept me going.

Sister Binkhurst was so supportive and helped me like no one else could. In her e-mails, she told me that I was smart and that I could do hard things. She also told me how proud she was of me. That helped tremendously. She even told me that Heavenly Father had sent her for me as a "helpmeet." She said she had found out that her purpose in life was to love me. I remember asking, "Your purpose is to love me?" I couldn't believe that God had someone just for me, someone sent to love me for who I am.

My goal in school was just to pass, but with all this help, I finished with a 3.8 grade-point average in my first semester. In the second semester, I achieved a 4.0! I totally blew myself away. During this time, I sacrificed a lot. I was on a tight budget and saving every dollar I could for a simple wedding. My heart wanted to give my bride a magnificent reception and honeymoon, but my budget couldn't buy much. Going to a plasma bank became a way for me to legally earn extra money for our wedding. It was a sacrifice I was willing to make, but I'm glad I didn't do it very long because it was unhealthy for me.

Bob and Marla, the couple who were with Sister Binkhurst when we first met, wanted to give us a very special wedding gift. They offered us a wedding reception and honeymoon! They even paid for the dress! I couldn't believe they could be so generous. I was astounded and hardly knew how to accept such incredible gifts.

I also wanted a better place for us to start our new life together. I was living in a small basement apartment. It was nice, and I appreciated it, but I wanted to give her something better. I also started to realize that I deserved better. We both wanted to be in an apartment building near Temple Square, but Sister Binkhurst didn't want to put any pressure on me. I wasn't receiving much from workers' compensation, and she knew that. I thought the building she liked was out of our budget, but when it comes to Heavenly Father, he makes anything possible.

With a heart full of hope, I put our name on a waiting list for an apartment. A unit became available soon after, but it was too expensive. I declined it and waited for another offer. I truly felt these apartments were where we were supposed to be.

Driving past the building one day, I said out loud, "Heavenly Father, we really want to live there, but if that's not

A Different Kind of Strong

where you want us to be, then bring us to where you would like us to be." A couple of hours later, I received an e-mail that another apartment was available. Even though this one was out of our budget as well, I knew the blessing was connected with accepting the will of the Father before my own.

Sister Binkhurst dreamed of having a view of the Salt Lake Temple, even if it was just a sliver of it. When I went to see the apartment, I walked out onto the community balcony just below the unit. There was a perfect view of the temple spires. It was beautiful—another amazing blessing! Heavenly Father was giving us everything our hearts desired.

CHAPTER 12

Finally and Forever

~~~

Toward the end of her mission, Sister Binkhurst began notifying her family and a few friends that we were going to be married soon after her return. I called her dad and asked for his blessing. I was also looking forward to talking with her mom and stepdad. The first time her mom and I talked, it was apparent that we were going to get along great. Her stepdad and I hit it off too. During the second phone call, I asked her mom if I could call her Mama. My new mama was so excited. Sister Binkhurst was an only child, and her mom had always wanted a son. They were both so glad to have one now.

Sister Binkhurst's mission came to an end. She flew back to California to be officially released from her mission call. Audrey and I decided to drive to California in order to be there for it. We stayed with Mama and Dad. We all got along great. It was like we had always been family.

The next day, the four of us met Sister Binkhurst at the airport. I was so happy to see her! She was still a set-apart missionary, so I couldn't give her a welcome-home hug yet.

I sat in the front seat of the car, and she sat in the back. We celebrated her return at her home teachers' house. Tom and Ilene have been, and continue to be, her church parents. Bob and Marla were there too! All of a sudden, I had several new parents. It was a nice and intimate reunion. We all got to know each other better.

We met the sister's stake president at the church. She told him our story and revealed that we were going to be married in six weeks. He was so surprised and said he had never experienced this as a stake president. A few close friends and family members were in the room. Everyone got to tell parts of our story. This event was recorded on video, thanks to Audrey. We love to watch it every now and again.

Finally came the moment we had been waiting for. As a released missionary, my fiancée was no longer Sister Binkhurst. We stood face-to-face for a few moments. I was a little anxious. I think we all were. Then, for the first time, we embraced. We both felt like we were finally home. I felt a huge relief. At last, I had found the one I had been looking for my entire life. I had always wanted a princess, even as a little boy. I had finally found her and was now hugging her—my princess, Julianne! We hugged for quite some time…so long that I think it made some people uncomfortable.

On the way back to her parents', we sat in the back seat together, getting as close to each other as we could. It felt wonderful. It was a dream come true.

That night, I took my fiancée out on our first date. Where do you think we went? We drove to an LDS church parking

Cant wait Bubba

lot. That's where she wanted to go. It was very romantic. We listened to music and danced under the stars together. We hugged, talked, and read letters to each other. These were not the regular letters we had written in our e-mails. They were special letters we had wanted each other to read after her mission.

The funniest thing happened while we were snuggling in the front seat. A cop pulled up and asked us what we were doing. It was hilarious! We felt like two teenagers getting busted for making out in the car, but we weren't making out. We had decided long before that our first real kiss wasn't going to happen until the day we were married. Our first date was wonderful and very memorable.

I stayed in California just for the weekend because I needed to return to school on Monday. I left the car with Julianne and Audrey and flew back to Salt Lake City. I focused on school and finishing my first semester strong. Once school ended, Julianne drove to Utah to pick me up. It was all very exciting!

With our wedding just a couple of weeks away, my dad decided to visit me on his way down to Los Angeles. It was great for Julianne to meet and get to know him. He brought a gift, a beautiful wood box he had made by hand at my request. This was a special box. Julianne had once given me a special box, and now I was returning the favor. This box would hold our love letters from her mission. We see it every day.

A Different Kind of Strong

During this time, we visited my cousins for a week. Our brief dating period was filled with spending time with family and attending Campus Education Week at BYU. Although we only went to three classes, it was fun being together. It didn't matter what we were doing, just as long as we were together.

The final week before our wedding, we did a lot of running around. It was exhausting. We didn't sleep much, but it was all worth it. I wasn't nervous at all. I knew that ours was a special kind of love. In 1 John 4:18, it says, "There is no fear in love; but perfect love casteth out fear: because fear hath torment. He that feareth is not made perfect in love." We were not afraid.

The night before the wedding, we stayed in two separate rooms at the Los Angeles Temple apartments. Julianne, Audrey, and another one of her friends were in one room, and I had another room down the hall. We were all in their room, picking out songs for the wedding. She was wondering what our first-dance song was going to be. Little did she know, I had already picked it. Actually, I had written a song for our first dance. I called it "Sunshine" because she was my sunshine.

There was a grassy area in front of my room. I grabbed a blanket and took Julianne outside. We sat and gazed at the temple. It was lit up beautifully! Wow, we were doing it. We were really going to be married and sealed the next day, for time and eternity.

The next morning, my parents arrived. It was the first time my mom and Julianne had met. What a wonderful moment that was for both of them. They got along instantly. Once we all got ready, we were off to the temple.

On August 30, 2014, we had a very intimate and sacred ceremony in the Los Angeles Temple. Our sealing was extra special because it was a "white wedding," where everyone was dressed in white clothing, even the guests. For this to happen, the temple matron needed to give her permission. To me, it was another sign from Heavenly Father that he wanted us to have everything.

I had always thought I would be sealed in the Salt Lake Temple, but I sacrificed my wants so that my bride could be sealed in the temple of her choice. However, we were informed that the altar in our sealing room was originally from the Salt Lake Temple. Isn't Heavenly Father amazing? He gave us both our wishes.

During our sealing, I was overwhelmed by many emotions. I felt joy and happiness. I thought of all the struggles I had endured to get where I was. I could not hold back the tears. I wept at the altar, looking across at my little princess. The spirit was strong. Family and friends were weeping. It felt so right. Then came the kiss, the kiss we had waited so long for. Soft, loving, and unforgettable. Then finally, it was official. We were going to be together forever.

When we came out of the temple, her family, my siblings, and more of our friends were waiting for us. It was great to see all the support we had. We took pictures and got to meet our new family members. We walked the temple grounds and felt the love of our Heavenly Father. These moments were something that you could not put a price on.

Our wedding reception was at our dear friends' home in Westlake Village. The setting was absolutely spectacular! Lee and Marti's house was elegant and the back garden stunning. We had a ring ceremony, and Julianne's bishop explained the meaning of the temple sealing for those guests who were not members of The Church of Jesus Christ of Latter-day Saints. My dad was the photographer and took over seven hundred pictures that day. One of my sisters made our wedding cake. It had beautiful olive branches shaped into a heart, symbolic of the Savior. <u>Everything was perfect.</u>

I surprised my bride with two songs. I had a guitar and played a song I had written about her called "Just My Size." She was petite, and that was just the perfect size for me. The song was also about the size of her heart. I didn't know how Heavenly Father put such a huge heart in such a small frame. I also played the song for our first dance, the one named "Sunshine." It was a magical moment! The entire reception was a dream. Everyone felt the love and the spirit there. They were all so happy for us.

Our honeymoon started in Westlake Village, continued in Hawaii, and was extended to Las Vegas. In Oahu, we stayed at a great hotel across the street from the beach. We visited the LDS Laie Hawaii Temple and the Polynesian Cultural Center. I had never been to the islands and couldn't think of a better time to go. This was the best vacation I had ever had.

A week later, we returned to California and packed Julianne's belongings into a small moving truck. Our honeymoon wasn't over yet. We were delayed in Las Vegas due to a flood that washed out the main highway. We had no choice but to stay in town.

We went out to dinner and decided to walk the Strip. As I mentioned before, I had lived in Vegas, but now the place felt different. As we walked the Strip, I started to feel sick to my stomach. I thought I might throw up—but not from being physically ill. Had I changed so much that I couldn't tolerate such an environment anymore? I looked around, and all I saw was sin. I felt I was being attacked spiritually, and it physically affected me. The feelings were so intense that we had to go back to the room. Once we did, the sickness departed. How interesting. What I used to think was cool and exciting I now found totally disgusting.

Due to many detours, it took us twenty hours to get back to Salt Lake. We were apart during that drawn-out drive home, as we were in two separate vehicles. Although the journey was long, we were happy, because we knew we were heading home: to a new life together, forever.

CHAPTER 13

THE REASONS FOR ADVERSITY

I LEARNED MANY LESSONS FROM adversity, which is meant to help us in several ways. President Howard W. Hunter said, "When [the difficulties of mortality] humble us and refine us and teach us and bless us, they can be powerful instruments in the hands of God to make us better people."[1] That brief sentence gives five positive outcomes of adversity. Number one is that it humbles us. Number two, it refines us. Three, it teaches us. Four, it blesses us. And number five declares that those difficulties can make us better people.

Let's go over all five. We will start with how adversity humbles us. To be humble is to be lowly and meek, poor in spirit, submissive, and teachable. Ether 12:27 says, "And if men come

---

1 Howard W. Hunter, "Adversity—Part of God's Plan for Our Eternal Progression," *Teachings of Presidents of the Church: Howard W. Hunter*, Salt Lake City: Intellectual Reserve, Inc., 2015, 61. https://www.lds.org/manual/teachings-of-presidents-of-the-church-howard-w-hunter/chapter-3-adversity-part-of-gods-plan-for-our-eternal-progress?lang=eng

Daniel L. Trotter

unto me I will show unto them their weakness. I give unto men weakness that they may be humble; and my grace is sufficient for all men that humble themselves before me; for if they humble themselves before me, and have faith in me, then will I make weak things become strong unto them."

Trials bring us to our knees and invite us to pray for help. It is during desperate times that we find the true meaning of humility. It means that we must become submissive like little children. This allows us to be teachable so that we can pray, act, and listen for answers. As we partake of this faith-filled lesson, we receive personal revelation, and doors open.

How does adversity refine us? By definition, to be refined is to be brought to a fine or a pure state—free from impurities. Wouldn't it be great to be free from impurities? Free of fear, corruption, and addiction? Fear is replaced with faith, corruption is turned into virtue, and addictions are transformed into self-mastery. Only through the help of the Godhead and opposition will we become like Them.

For instance, think about the forging of a samurai sword. You start out with raw, simple material just like we are. That solid material is then heated and shaped into a long, lean block of metal, which is then cooled. The metal, or the human soul, is now ready for the sixteen-hundred-degree furnace. Here come the trials.

The extreme heat makes the material flexible for shaping and helps remove impurities, or our imperfections. Sulfur and silica are separated from the iron and create slag. Slag is the more or less completely fused and vitrified matter separated during the reduction of a metal from its ore. So there must be a separation. The types of matter cannot remain together if you want the raw metal to become a samurai sword.

The heated material is pulled from the furnace once it becomes a glowing, yellowish-orange color. The metal is now pliable. Elder Quentin L. Cook said, "The refiner's fire is real, and qualities of character and righteousness that are forged in the furnace of affliction perfect and purify us and prepare us to meet God."[2]

To forge the steel, the ironworker places it on an anvil and strikes it with life's sometimes brutal hammer. Blow after blow, the sword is shaped differently after each strike. As the sword begins to cool off, it loses its ability to be shaped. The ironworker thrusts the premature sword back into the furnace so that it can be fashioned closer to what it must become.

Just like in life, the sword gets a break. But for not too long. Although things have cooled down, the transformation is still not complete. A dull sword does a samurai no good. Out come the grinder and files. Back and forth, the ironworker grinds and files the metal to form the final shape of the blade. Now it's time for it to be treated.

A special clay mixture is added in order to achieve the desired results. The spine of the blade is coated with the mixture. This makes the spine flexible and leaves the edge of the blade sharp. But the sword is not done yet. Back into the furnace it goes.

---

2 Quentin L. Cook, "The Songs They Could Not Sing," *Liahona* and *Ensign*, November 2011, 106. https://www.lds.org/general-conference/2011/10/the-songs-they-could-not-sing?lang=eng

After the reheating process, the steel needs to be quenched. The change in temperature cools and hardens the substance. It is placed in water or oil along the edge and tip first. There are two reasons that this is done. First, to make the cutting surface as hard as it can be. Second, it keeps the back of the blade softer to absorb the blows delivered by adversaries. The faster the quenching process, the harder the sword becomes.

Time for the blade to be tempered. This takes less heat. The blade is reheated to four hundred degrees, and then like us, if we choose, it surrenders to the creator and the environment as it cools to room temperature. This creates a balance of flexibility and firmness. Just a few more final changes, and the sword will be ready to battle the enemy.

The clay is then removed, and the edge of the blade is ground until sharp. The sword now needs to be perfected by detailing the rough areas. The edge of the blade is then fully sharpened with a water stone. Images of baptism and granite temples come to mind. After the polishing is complete, the blade is now perfectly balanced.

The handle, or hilt, of the blade is created with an end cap and must be long enough to accommodate both hands to provide optimal balance and added protection. The two hands symbolize Heavenly Father and the Savior guiding the direction of their creation. The *tsuba*, or hand guard (representing our covenants), is placed at the bottom of the blade to protect the hands from incoming enemy strikes. The samurai sword has now reached perfection and is finally complete.

Can we really be made perfect? That depends on what our definition of perfect is. If it means that we will never make mistakes again, I would have to say no. We cannot be perfect like that in this life. But if it means that when we make a mistake, we repent, try to make things right, do our best to not do those things again, and use the atonement, then I would say yes. We can be made perfect. (By the way, the word *perfect* in several scriptures means "complete.")

Back to the reasons for adversity. In Isaiah 48:10, we read, "Behold, I have refined thee, but not with silver; I have chosen thee in the furnace of affliction." We all go through the refiner's fire. Why? For His sake and for our eternal benefit.

How does adversity teach us? In order for us to learn, we must become teachable, which refers us back to being humble. Doctrine and Covenants 104:79 states, "And it is my will that you shall humble yourselves before me, and obtain this blessing by your diligence and humility and the prayer of faith."

In a First Presidency message, President James E. Faust said, "Many in today's generation have not fully known nor appreciated the refining blessings of adversity. Many have never been hungry because of want. Yet I am persuaded that there can be a necessary refining process in adversity that increases our understanding, enhances our sensitivity, and makes us more Christlike."[3] President Faust then asks two significant questions: "Why is adversity often such a good

---

3 James E. Faust, "The Blessings of Adversity," *Ensign*, February 1998, 2. https://www.lds.org/ensign/1998/02/the-blessings-of-adversity?lang=eng

schoolmaster? Is it because it teaches so many things?" He answers, "Through difficult circumstances we are often forced to learn discipline and how to work. In often unpleasant circumstances we may also be subjected to a buffeting, a honing, and a polishing that can come no other way." Between the raw material, the ironworker, the heat, the anvil, the hammer, the clay, and the water comes a beautiful weapon against the evils of the world. If we let God refine us and teach us, we can be that weapon against evil.[4]

Trials also bless us in many ways. While the prophet Joseph Smith was in Liberty Jail, he pleaded with the Lord for help for the saints and for himself. The Lord's response to his prayer is in Doctrine and Covenants 121:7–8: "My son, peace be unto thy soul; thine adversity and thine afflictions shall be but a small moment; and then, if thou endure it well, God shall exalt thee on high; thou shalt triumph over all thy foes."

Notice how the Lord gives the prophet a blessing that will not take place in his lifetime. It is to come in the next life. I don't know about you, but there are times when I want immediate blessings. The world has become obsessed with instant gratification. We want everything now.

Elder Jeffrey R. Holland of the Quorum of the Twelve Apostles declares, "They [meaning the Father and the Son] sustain us in our hour of need—and always will, even if we cannot recognize that intervention. Some blessings come soon, some come late, and some don't come until heaven;

---

4 Ibid., 5.

but for those who embrace the gospel of Jesus Christ, *they come*."⁵ As Latter-day Saints, we are reminded to focus on the eternal perspective.

Elder Robert D. Hales of the Quorum of the Twelve Apostles says, "In the school of mortality, the tutor is often pain and tribulation, but the lessons are meant to refine and bless us and strengthen us, not to destroy us. There is nothing that we are enduring that Jesus does not understand, and He waits for us to go to our Heavenly Father in prayer. I testify that if we will be obedient and if we are diligent, our prayers will be answered, our problems will diminish, our fears will dissipate, light will come upon us, the darkness of despair will be dispersed, and we will be close to the Lord and feel of His love and of the comfort of the Holy Ghost."⁶

What wonderful promised blessings from an apostle of the Lord. Prayers will be answered, problems diminished, fears dissolve, light will come upon us, and the darkness of despair, even depression, can be dispersed and healed. Then comes the ultimate payoff: to be close to the Lord, feel His love, and be comforted by the Holy Ghost. That sings peace to my soul.

Our trials can also become powerful instruments in the hands of God, instruments that can make us better people. Why is it that the Savior can help us like no one else can?

---

5 Jeffrey R. Holland, "An High Priest of Good Things to Come," *Ensign*, November 1999, 38. https://www.lds.org/general-conference/1999/10/an-high-priest-of-good-things-to-come?lang=eng

6 Robert D. Hales, "Faith Trough Tribulation Brings Peace and Joy," *Ensign*, May 2003, 17. https://www.lds.org/general-conference/2003/04/faith-through-tribulation-brings-peace-and-joy?lang=eng

Because unlike anyone else, He has been there, done that. He knows what it is like to be all of us. He knows what you and I have been through, and He knows how to heal us.

Don't we relate better to people who have gone through similar trials? I'm not saying that people who have never been addicts can't help addicts. Individuals who have been clean their whole lives are helping addicts put back the pieces of their scattered puzzles. But the Savior, He gets it. He not only understands us, but He knows us better than we know ourselves.

So our experiences can help people. The challenges that we have gone through bless our lives and give us the opportunity to bless the lives of others. We can become powerful instruments in the hands of God because of them. Let us not be afraid to share the answers we have discovered that will help others with the challenges we have already faced.

Seven Steps to Freedom - Ways to Overcome Adversity and Addiction, and Find Peace and Happiness

1. **Prayer**
   Prayer takes faith and starts the process. We are asking for help beyond our own capabilities. As we know, faith without works is dead, so after we pray, we need

to take action. When we become proactive, God's response is definite.

2. **Repentance**

   Part 1: Asking God for forgiveness

   Repentance is more than just feeling sorry for what we have done. We must confess our sins, ask God to forgive us, and try our best to sin no more. That means keeping the commandments the best we can. Repentance is also about correcting the problems our actions have caused. This takes honesty and humility. Most important, repentance is knowing that forgiveness is possible because of the atonement of Jesus Christ. Through Him, all things are possible. Remember that repentance is a process and takes time, so be patient with yourself.

   Part 2: Forgiving others

   In a conference talk, Elder Kevin R. Duncan of the Seventy said, "Gratefully, God, in His love and mercy for His children, has prepared a way to help us navigate these sometimes turbulent experiences of life. He has provided an escape for all who fall victim to the misdeeds of others. He has taught us that we can forgive! Even though we may be a victim once, we need not be a victim twice by carrying the burden of hate, bitterness, pain, resentment, or even revenge. We can forgive, and we can be free!"[7]

Part 3: Forgiving ourselves

This might be the hardest one for us to do. Why is this so challenging? I believe it's because Satan continually reminds us of our wrongdoings. When we listen to the Adversary and negative self-talk, our progression stops, and we lose intelligence. From my experience, I noticed that the closer I came to God and understood that He had forgiven me, the easier it was for me to forgive myself and be at peace.

3. **Counseling**

We are not meant to do this on our own. Psychologists and counselors can be beneficial and are recommended, but they do not have the authority to forgive sin. The repentance process must go through the proper priesthood channels. Go see your bishop. He is a judge in Israel and can forgive you on behalf of Heavenly Father and the Savior.

4. **Scripture study**

Become a daily partaker of His word. In my story, I said that the world had no answers for me. I had to go to the source and to the scriptures. I have found more answers in scriptures than all the other books I have read combined. Maybe that's not saying much,

---

7   Kevin R. Duncan, "The Healing Ointment of Forgiveness," *Liahona*, May 2016, 33. https://www.lds.org/general-conference/2016/04/the-healing-ointment-of-forgiveness?lang=eng&_r=1

but I know that the scriptures are true and have the answers for all the world's problems.

5. **Stand in holy places**

   1 Thessalonians 5:22–23 says, "Abstain from all appearance of evil. And the very God of peace sanctify you wholly; and I pray God your whole spirit and soul and body be preserved blameless unto the coming of our Lord Jesus Christ." Our minds are easily influenced, so be conscious of the things you do. Ask yourself, "If the Savior were here, would I be watching this movie or program? If the Savior were here, would I be listening to this music? If the Savior were here, what kind of language and tone would I use? If I were going to visit the Savior, what would I wear? Do the things I give my attention to bring me closer to the Savior?" As you ask yourself these questions be honest with your answers.

6. **Physical health**

   The healthiest thing we can do is live the gospel. Following the Word of Wisdom is not simply for good physical health, it is also vital for spiritual well-being. Therefore, we need to be mindful and put good things into our body. As we do, we will be able to feel the Holy Spirit more. The healthiest thing we can do nutritionally is eat more raw organic fruits and vegetables and minimize our intake of processed foods. In general, we really do not understand the negative effects processed foods have on our mental and physical health.

Let's talk about exercise. Exercise is good for the body when done properly. It helps us to maintain a healthy weight and gives us sustainable energy. Interval training is the healthiest form of exercise I have found, and it only takes fifteen minutes a day. Exercise is not about doing more; it's about being smart at what you do. Exercise is also good for the brain. It reduces depression and anxiety. Are you starting to see the importance of the mind, body, and spirit? It's all connected.

7. **Temple attendance**

All of the steps above lead directly to the temple. It is the portal for us to return to Heavenly Father. It is the most peaceful place on earth and helps us to receive personal revelation. It also gives us the opportunity to serve and help our ancestors receive ordinances that only the living can do. And remember, to get a temple recommend, we just need to be worthy—not perfect.

In times of hardship, I know it can be difficult to see the good in the struggle. We always want things to go smoothly. It's in our nature to think that way. But if in those moments we can take the time to breathe and be still, we can learn the lessons and teachings of the affliction. I know it's hard, but let's do our best to be patient. It's part of the process of becoming Christlike.

Be still... embrace your pain

I would like to leave you with a scripture. Alma 36:27 declares, "And I have been supported under trials and troubles of every kind, yea, and in all manner of afflictions; yea, God has delivered me from prison, and from bonds, and from death; yea, and I do put my trust in him, and he will still deliver me."

I testify that God lives and Jesus is the Christ. The atonement is real, and I am a witness of its power to heal. The gospel has been restored through the prophet Joseph Smith. I know the Book of Mormon is true and gives us answers. I also know that President Thomas S. Monson is a prophet of God and leads us in these latter days. May we all choose the will of our Heavenly Father, change our ways, and become the magnificent sons and daughters we are all meant to be. I testify that there is no other way. In the name of Jesus Christ, amen.

AFTERWORD
by Julianne Binkhurst Trotter

DANIEL IS A LIVING, BREATHING, walking, talking miracle! Now you know his story of triumph over trial. Overcoming several addictions, physical suffering, psychological warfare, homelessness, family separation, divorce, deep depression, hopelessness, attempted suicide, time in jail, and much more is miraculous. Wouldn't you agree? I marvel at the thought of who he is now and what he has become. He is an uncommon, unknown success story. In a crowd, you wouldn't be able to tell or even imagine his life's experiences and challenges.

Today Daniel is free from *all* his past dependencies. He has a clear mind, healthy body, positive outlook on life, and grateful attitude. He is not a victim but a victor! He is not only an overcomer, but he is also an achiever. He has learned the meaning of choice, responsibility, determination, discipline, and empowerment. He has become a master of change and self-improvement through awareness, obedience, and consistency. He is learning that he can do hard things—very hard things! He is exceeding all expectations he had for himself, and some that he never had at all. Even though Daniel barely graduated high school, he now has a college degree in information technology, graduating with a 3.92 GPA.

If you still ask yourself what the reasons were for Daniel's life challenges, here is the answer: God loves Daniel. All the events of his life were necessary to bring him to appreciate the here and now, because now is great! Now is real. Now is true. The real and good things in his life are not fleeting. They are permanent and everlasting. Why? Because they are grounded in the truth of God.

This simple yet almighty three-letter word holds the key to everything—yes, everything! Let me be very precise about this idea of God. He is the Father of us all, every single one of us. We may not know Him, but He absolutely knows us, individually and intimately. He loves each of us deeply. The evidence of Him and His love for us is Jesus Christ. So the reason for all of the adversity in Daniel's life is simply *love*.

Our Heavenly Father has always loved Daniel, but Daniel hasn't always loved Him. Daniel also didn't know for himself how much God loved him. He knows now and cannot deny it. With this knowledge of Father's patient and pure love for him, Daniel understands that miracles such as his come at a great price and with great responsibility. The price of freedom from his pains and addictions, his bondage, was paid dearly by Jesus Christ. This feeling of complete freedom came through many miracles, both small and enormous.

A Different Kind of Strong

The responsibility to give back and help others is a symbol of gratitude and love, a gift Daniel gladly offers.

I celebrate Daniel's life every day as well as my own. I am grateful for the beginning of our new life together as a married and sealed couple. I love Daniel and the wonderful wisdom he brings to our relationship. We invite God, our Father, and Jesus Christ into our lives every day. We open our hearts, hands, and home to Them. We continue to see miracles around us all the time, sometimes even within ourselves.

I, too, have been impacted by the knowledge of God's loving care and concern for me. I cannot deny that He also loves me. This understanding has brought me to my knees many times. I have learned it is only when we turn to our Heavenly Father, when we really want to change our lives for good and have the yearning desire to return to our Father's presence, that we begin to do whatever it takes to feel His love for us.

I know all these things are possible and true. I hope you may have a great desire to know these truths for yourself. God, our Father in heaven, does exist. His love for us is real. We are His children. He wants us to have true and eternal happiness. Seek this truth, and "seek this Jesus." He will set you free—free from whatever your bondage may be. With that new freedom, what will you do?

Now you know that a complete change is possible. It was possible for Daniel, it was possible for me, and it is possible for you. So what is keeping you from your great new life?

All you need to do to begin is pause and turn toward God. Before you know it, your heart will guide you closer to Him. Only there will you find what all of us are looking for—pure, unconditional, and unending love. Let your feet follow the direction of your heart as you begin to turn to God and Jesus Christ. It is only when we understand and accept His atonement that we truly begin to change and grow strong. Find comfort, healing, strength, and peace in His ultimate gift of love. Come back to Him, and discover for yourself a different kind of strong.

Discover More Today

- Visit the website to receive your bonus gift!
  - **Enjoy a FREE song.**
- Follow Daniel on Social Media
  - Become a fan on Facebook facebook.com/danielltrotter
  - Stay tuned on YouTube
- Schedule Daniel for a corporate event
- Share your story! What have you overcome with God's help?

www.DanielLTrotter.com

AUTHOR BIO

AUTHOR AND MOTIVATIONAL SPEAKER DANIEL L. Trotter is the founder of Absolute Fitness Empowerment Center, an integrated gym and wellness facility. As a certified fitness trainer and specialist in performance nutrition, Daniel advocates for holistic wellness, inside and out, from clean eating to physical fitness.

Daniel is also a singer and songwriter who encourages people to seek a relationship with Jesus Christ through his uplifting talks and musical performances.

Daniel and his wife, Julianne, can often be found at a transitional center operated by The Church of Jesus Christ of Latter-Day Saints that serves the chronically homeless of downtown Salt Lake City.

Made in the USA
Lexington, KY
20 April 2018